A Funny Year in the Garden

Gardening Cartoons
by

Chris Madden

INKLINE PRESS

A FUNNY YEAR IN THE GARDEN
Gardening Cartoons by Chris Madden

Copyright © 2006 Chris Madden

ISBN: 0-9548551-2-4

Published by Inkline Press
www.inklinepress.com

SPRING

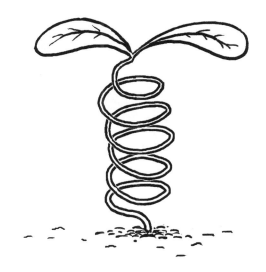

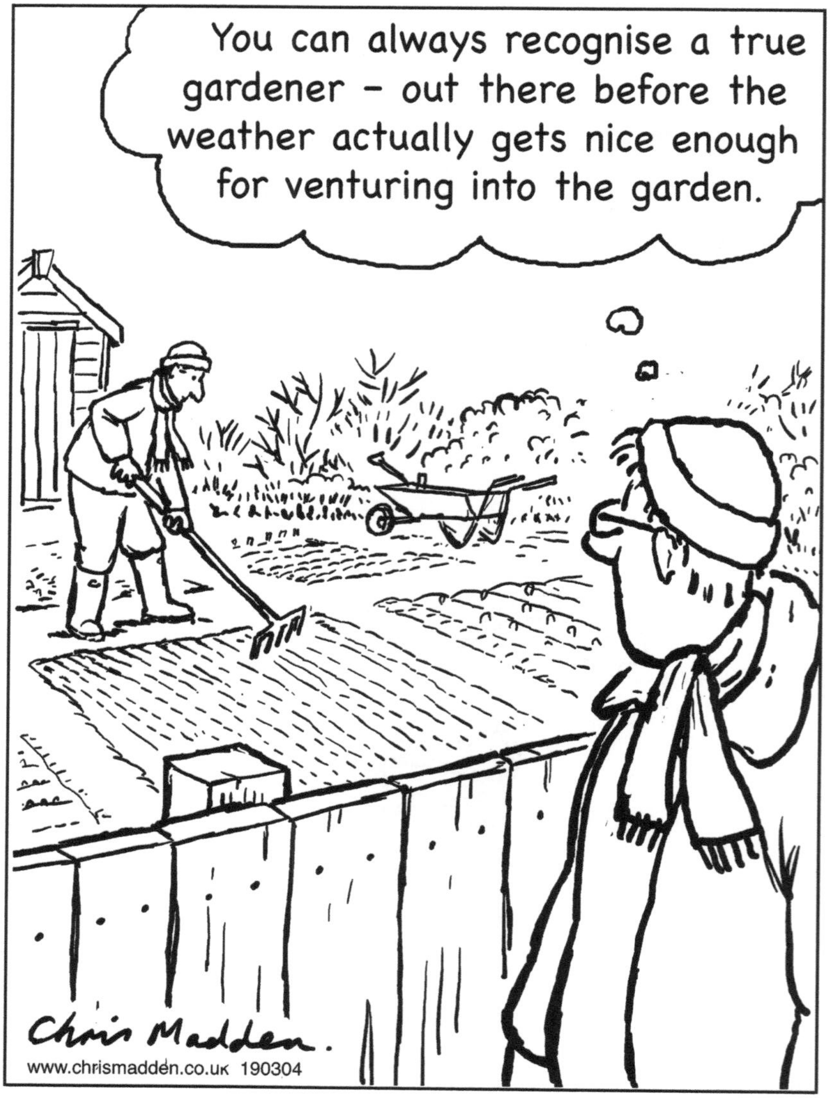
You can always recognise a true gardener - out there before the weather actually gets nice enough for venturing into the garden.
Chris Madden.
www.chrismadden.co.uk 190304

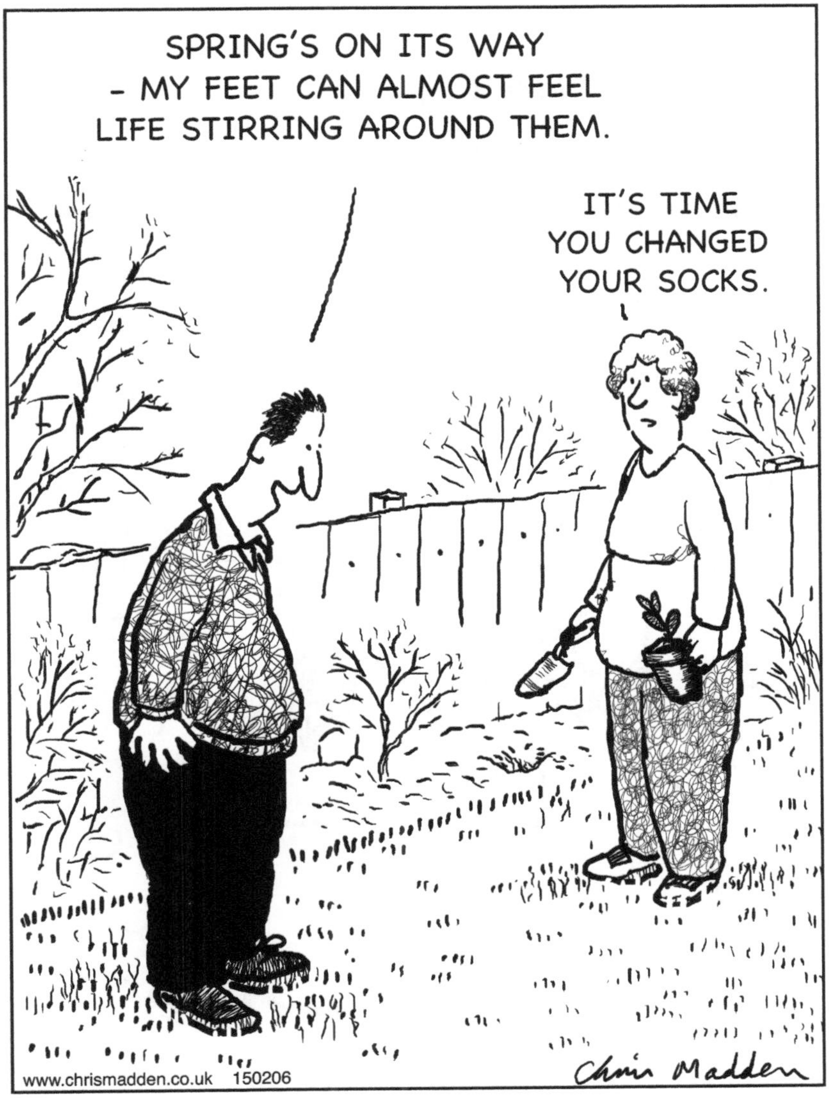
SPRING'S ON ITS WAY - MY FEET CAN ALMOST FEEL LIFE STIRRING AROUND THEM.
IT'S TIME YOU CHANGED YOUR SOCKS.
www.chrismadden.co.uk 150206
Chris Madden

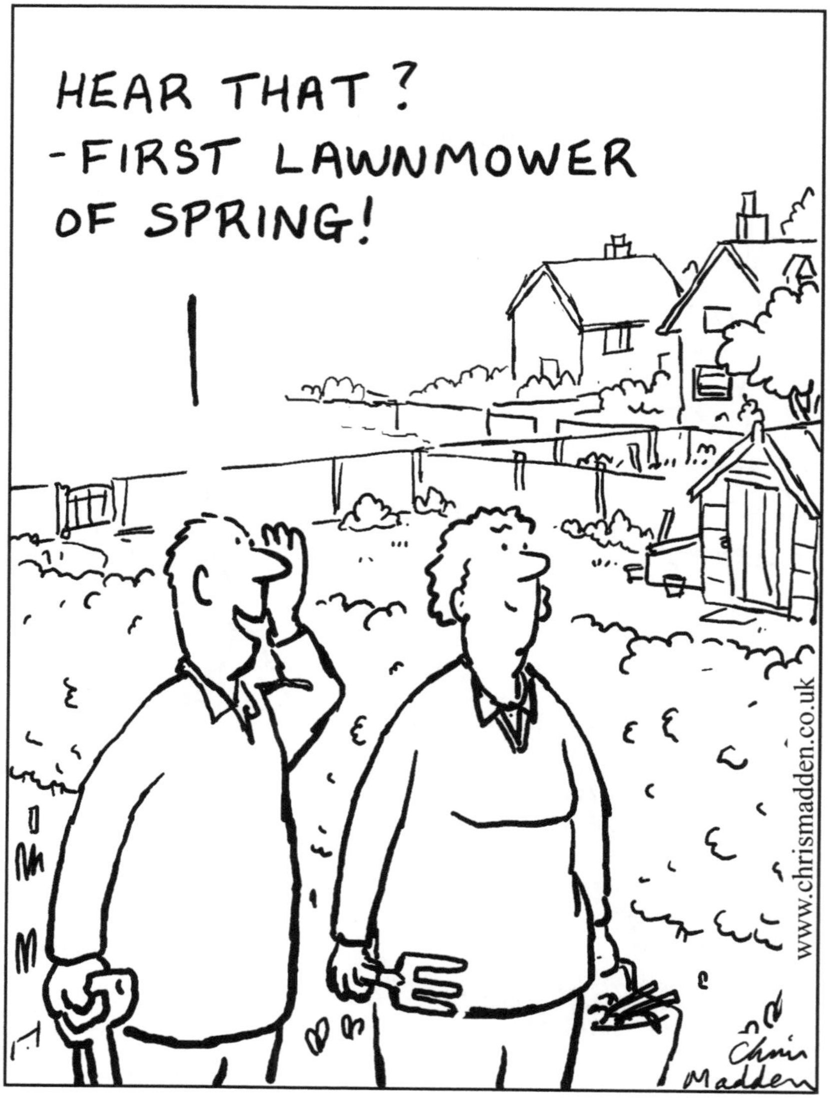
HEAR THAT ?
-FIRST LAWNMOWER
OF SPRING!
www.chrismadden.co.uk
Chris
Madden

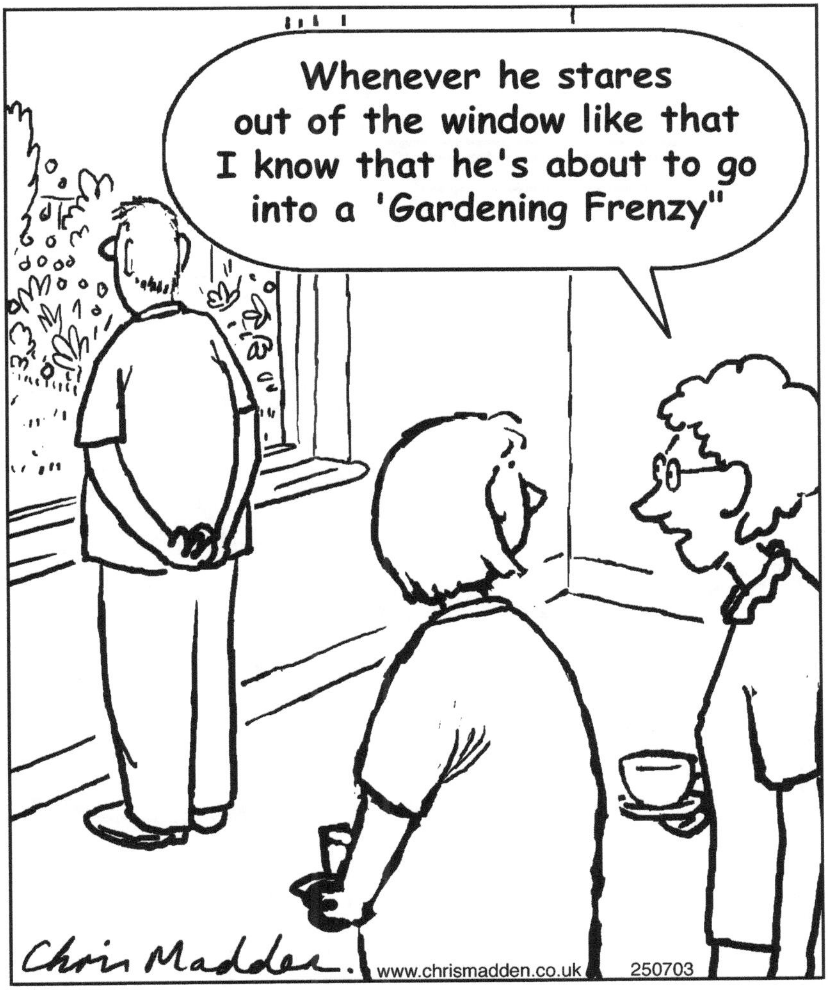
Whenever he stares out of the window like that I know that he's about to go into a 'Gardening Frenzy"
Chris Madden.
www.chrismadden.co.uk
250703

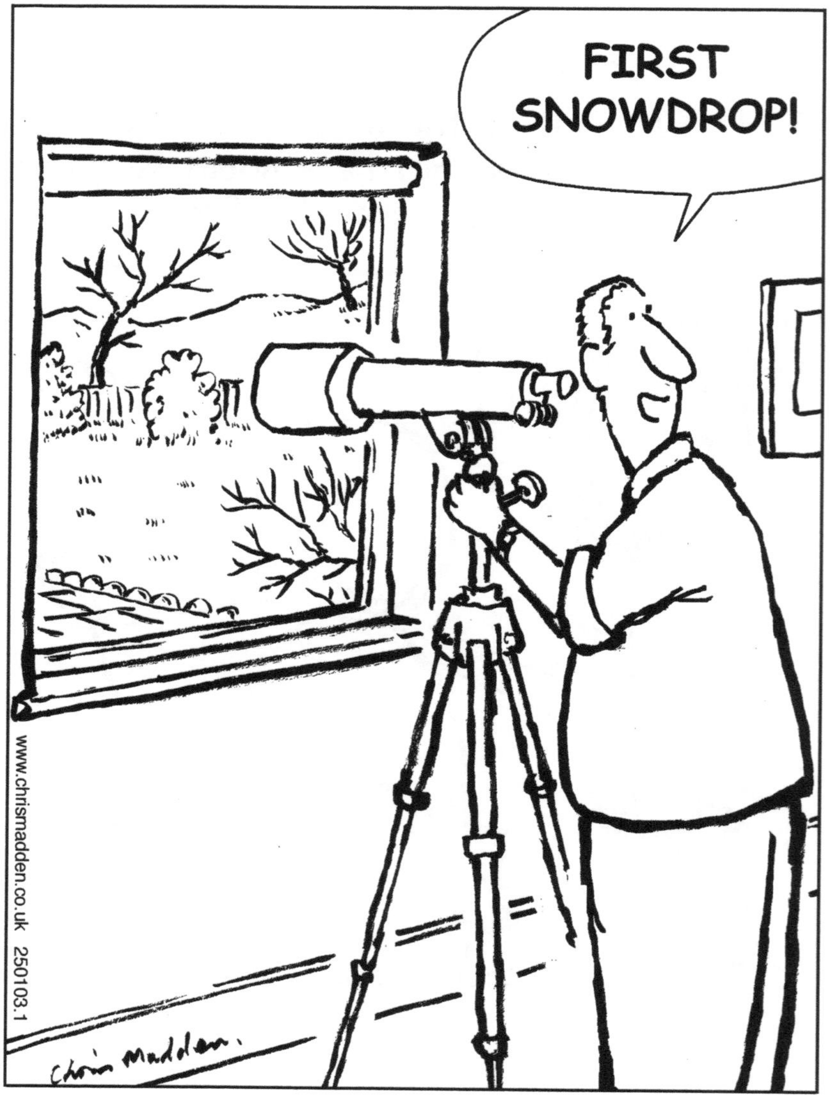
FIRST SNOWDROP!
www.chrismadden.co.uk 250103.1
Chris Madden

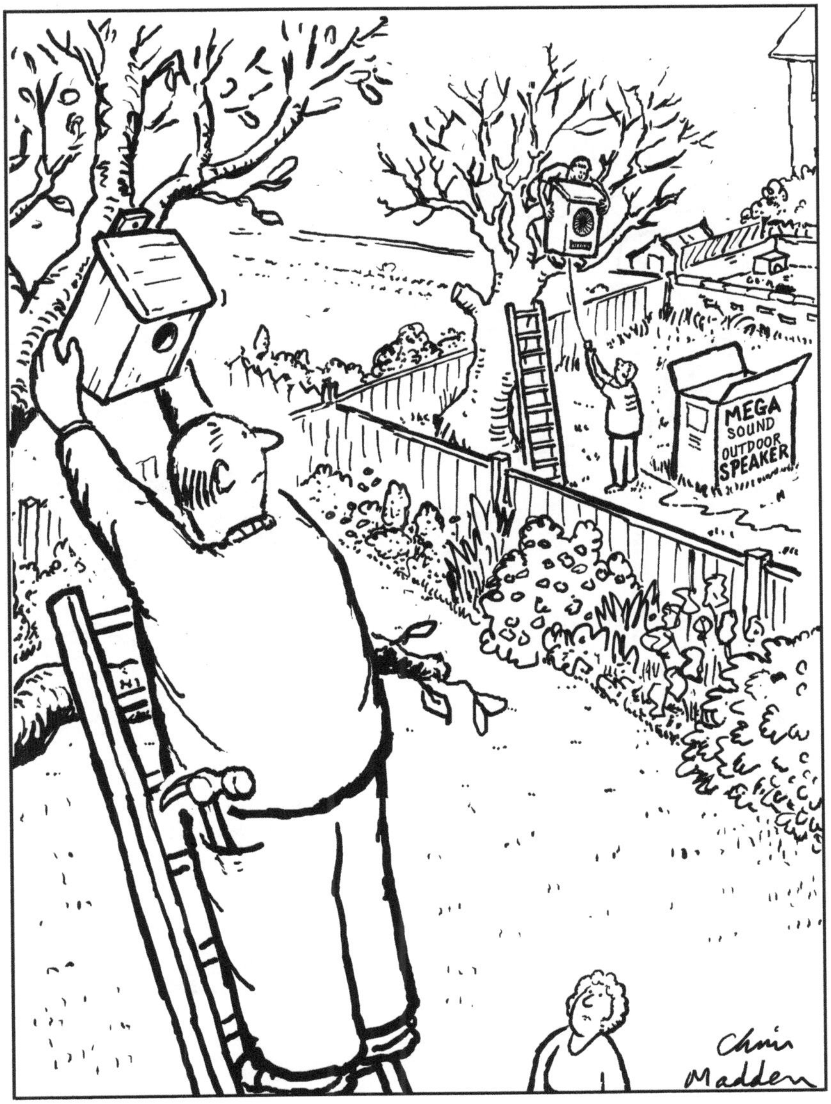
MEGA
SOUND
OUTDOOR
SPEAKER
Chris
Madden

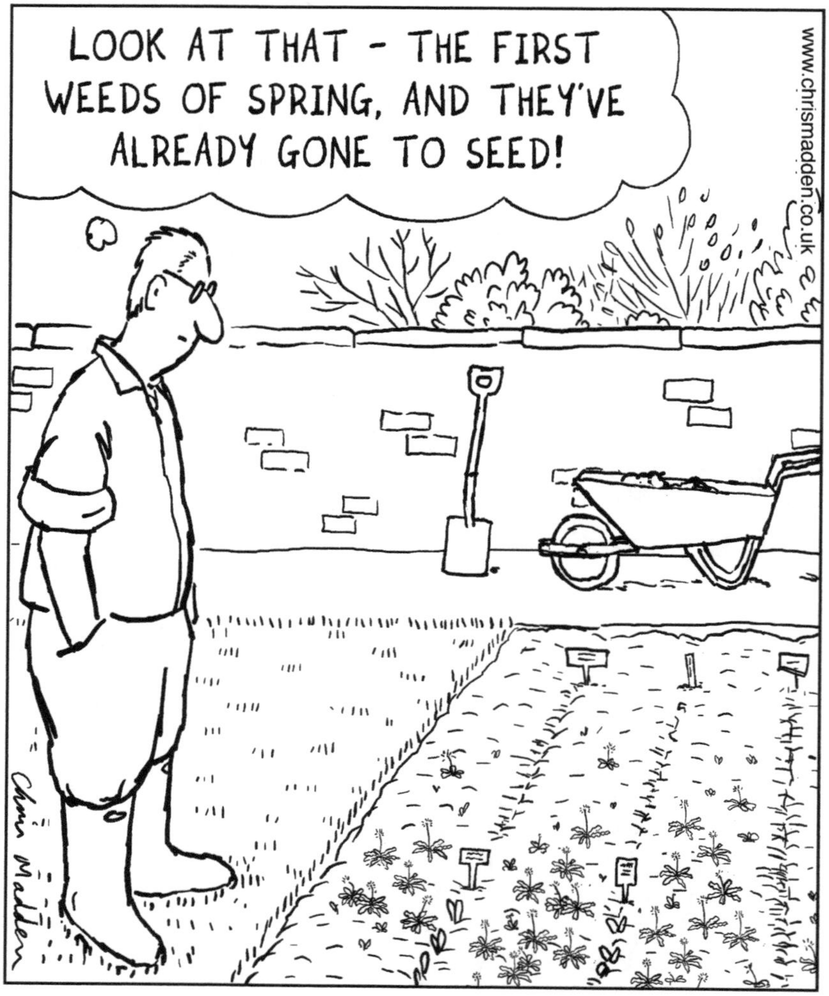
LOOK AT THAT - THE FIRST WEEDS OF SPRING, AND THEY'VE ALREADY GONE TO SEED!
www.chrismadden.co.uk
Chris Madden

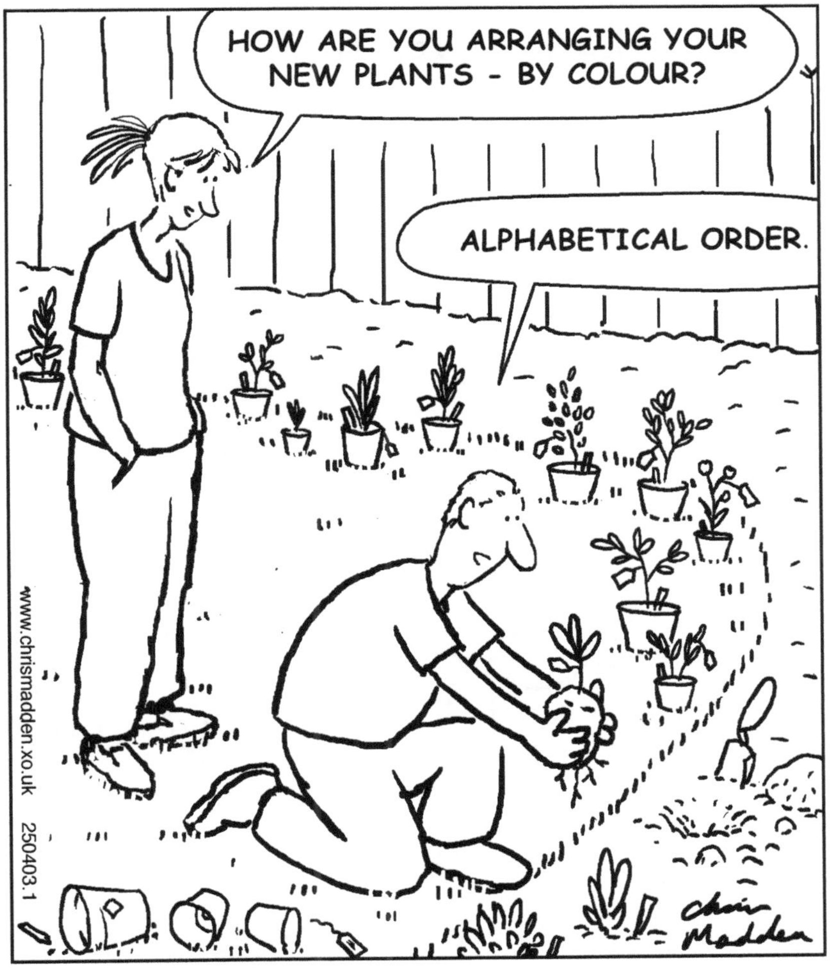
HOW ARE YOU ARRANGING YOUR NEW PLANTS - BY COLOUR?
ALPHABETICAL ORDER.
www.chrismadden.xo.uk 250403.1
Chris Madden

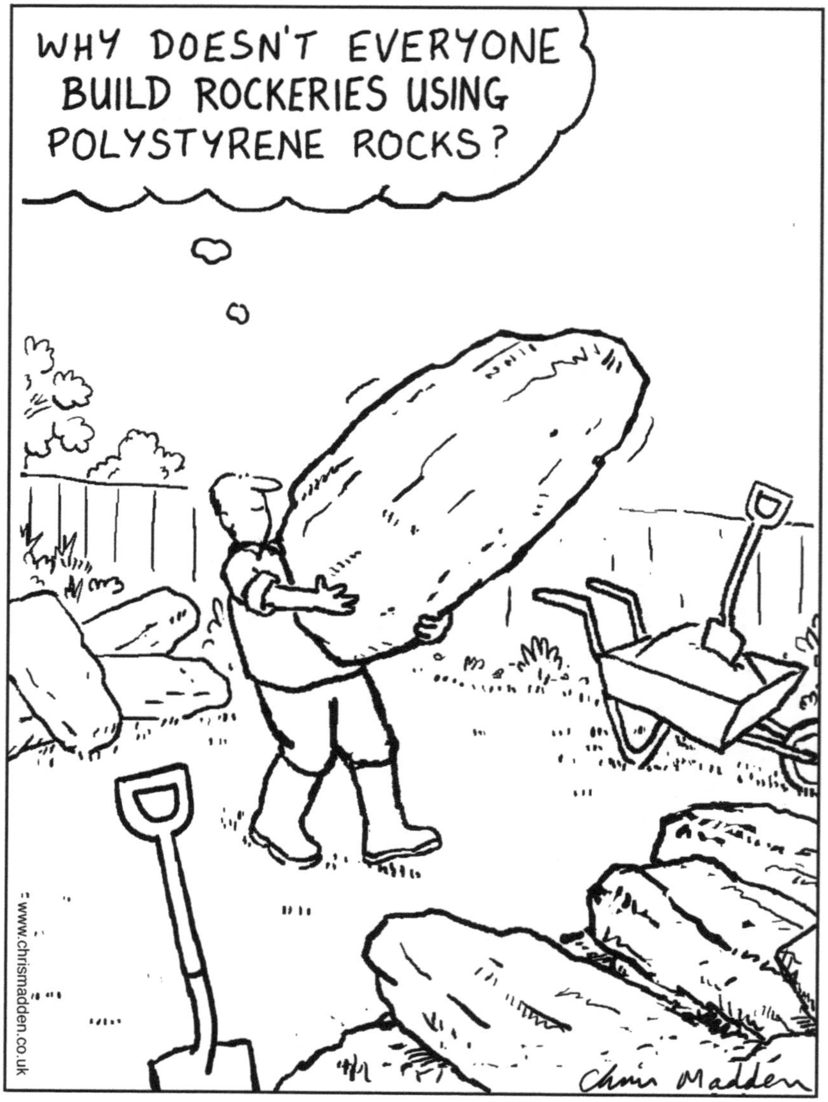
WHY DOESN'T EVERYONE BUILD ROCKERIES USING POLYSTYRENE ROCKS?
www.chrismadden.co.uk
Chris Madden

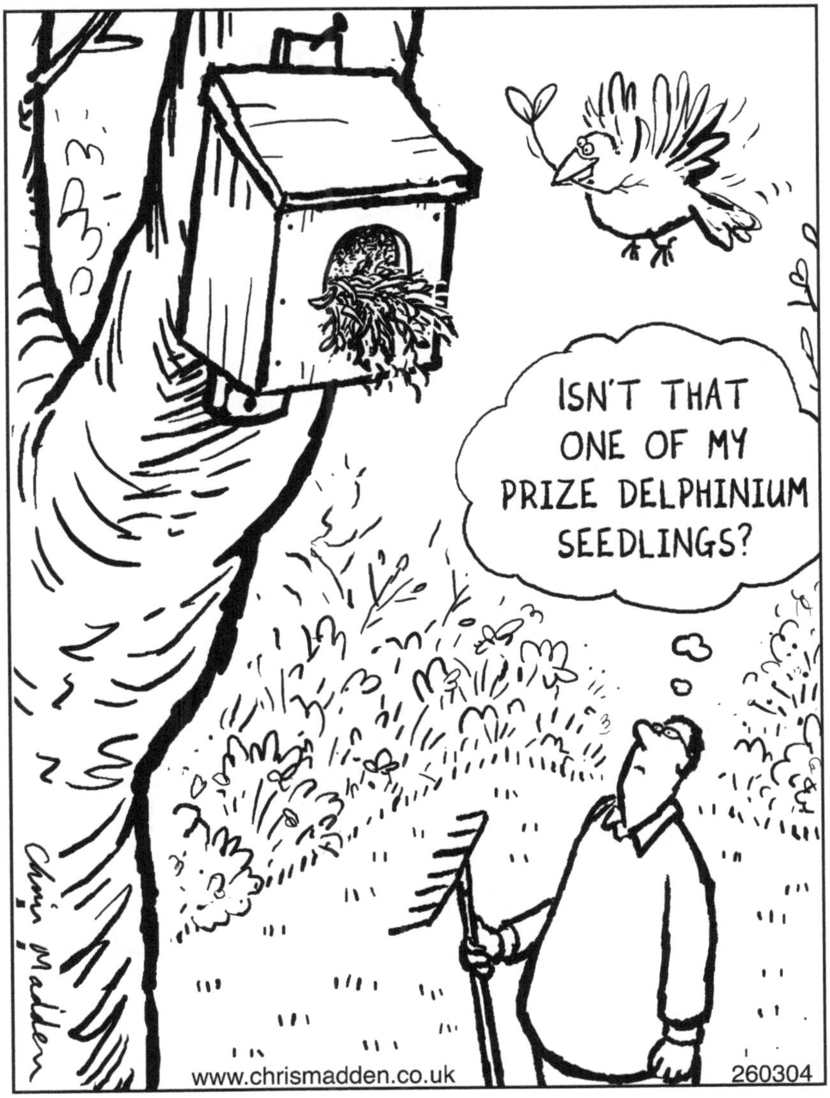
ISN'T THAT ONE OF MY PRIZE DELPHINIUM SEEDLINGS?
Chris Madden
www.chrismadden.co.uk
260304

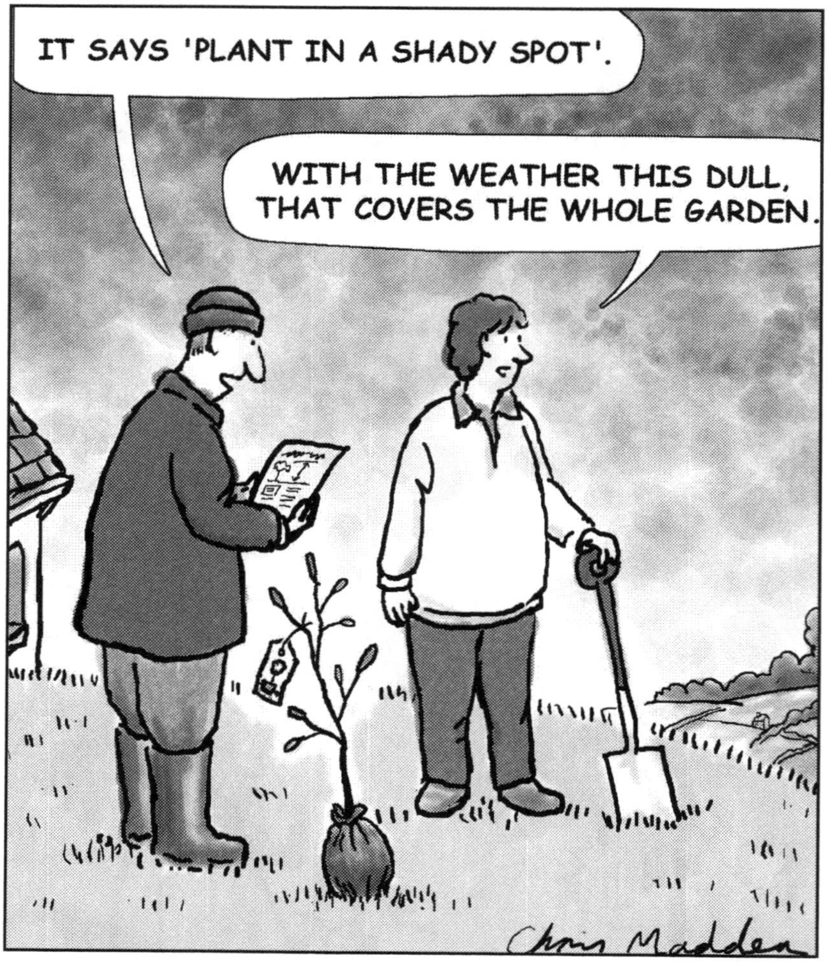
IT SAYS 'PLANT IN A SHADY SPOT'.
WITH THE WEATHER THIS DULL, THAT COVERS THE WHOLE GARDEN.
Chris Madden

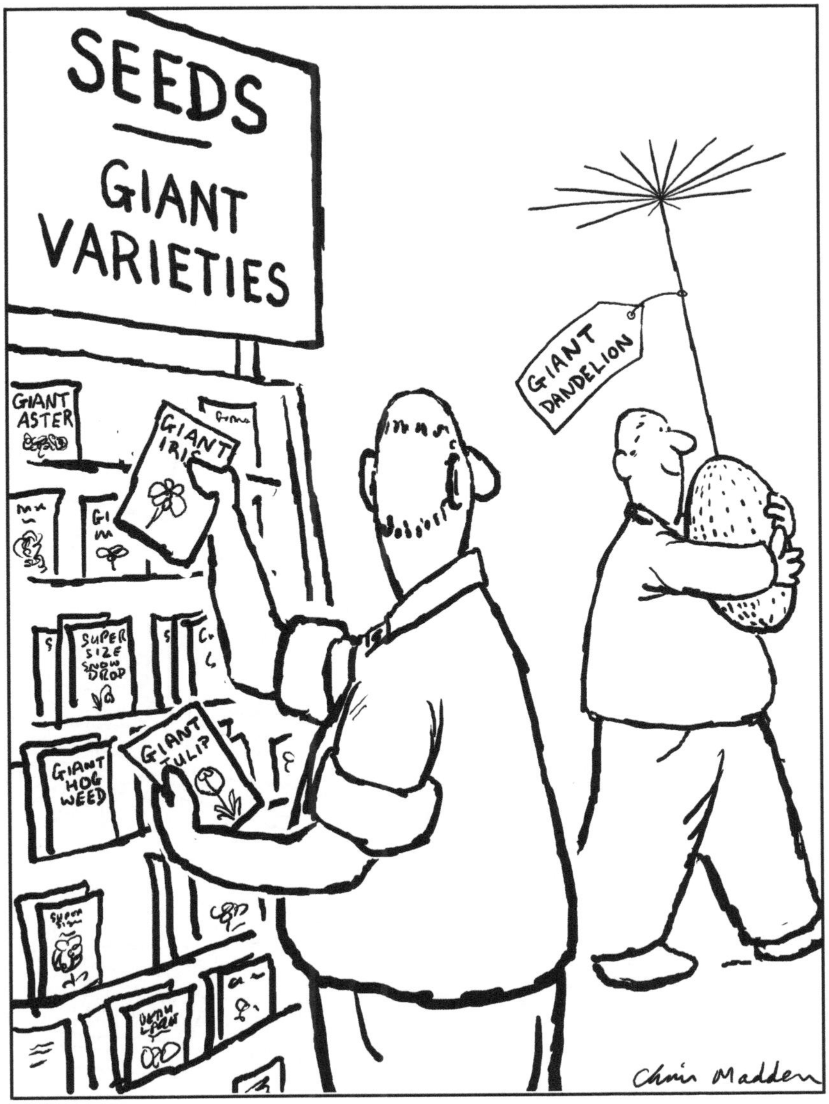
SEEDS
GIANT VARIETIES
GIANT ASTER
GIANT IRIS
SUPER SIZE SNOW DROP
GIANT HOG WEED
GIANT TULIP
GIANT DANDELION
Chris Madden

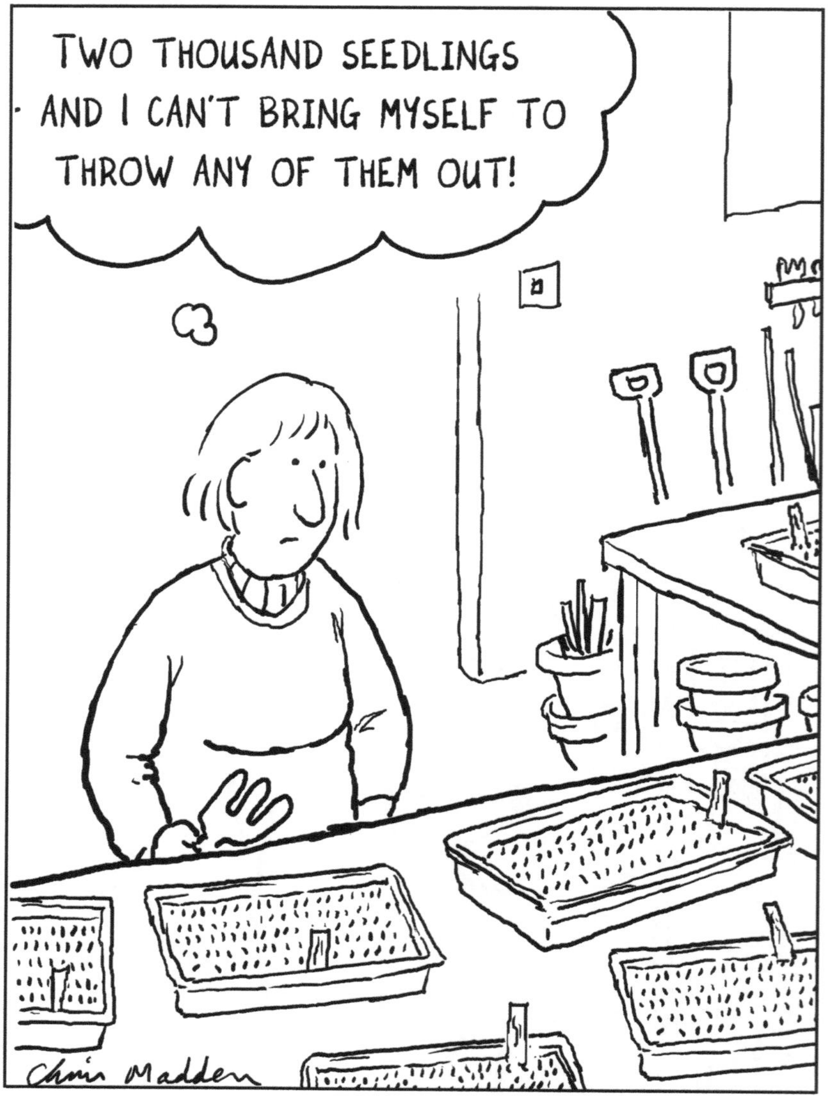
TWO THOUSAND SEEDLINGS AND I CAN'T BRING MYSELF TO THROW ANY OF THEM OUT!
Chris Madden

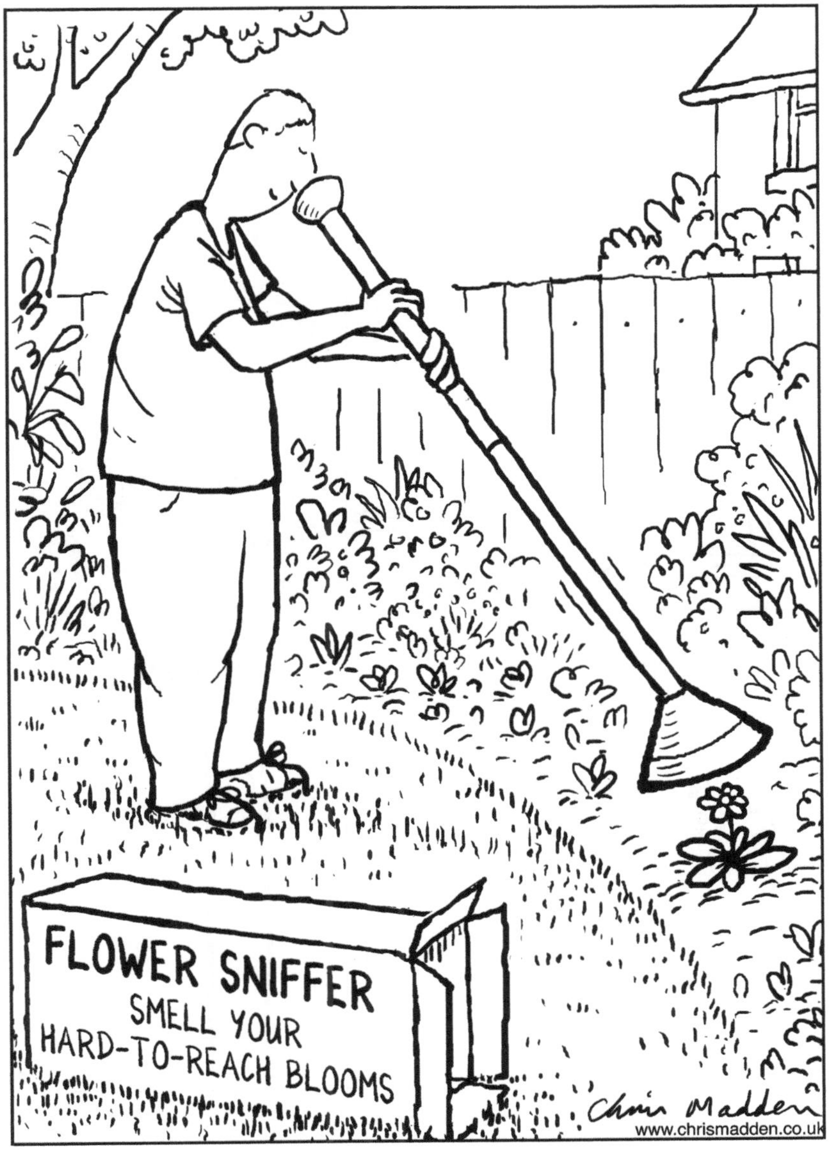
FLOWER SNIFFER
SMELL YOUR
HARD-TO-REACH BLOOMS
Chris Madden
www.chrismadden.co.uk

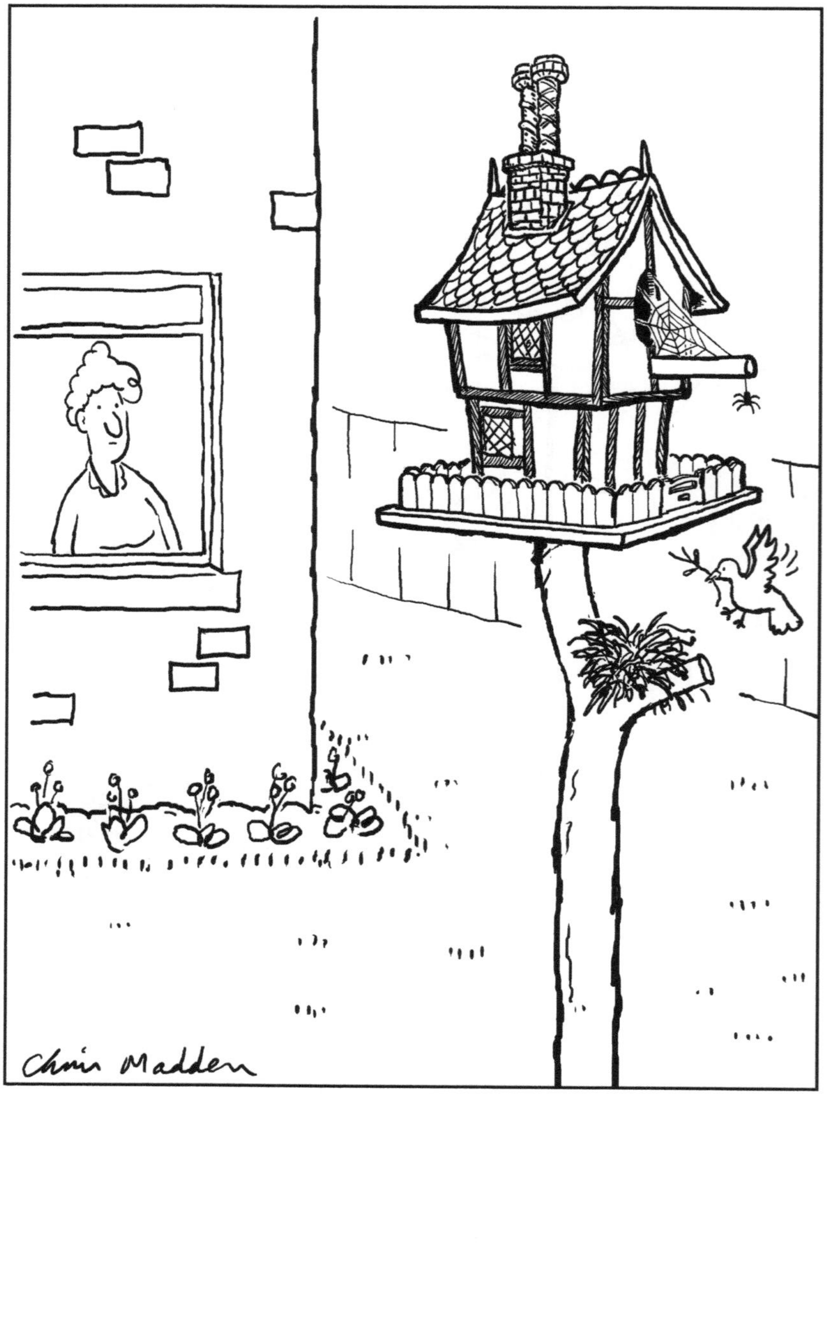
Chris Madden

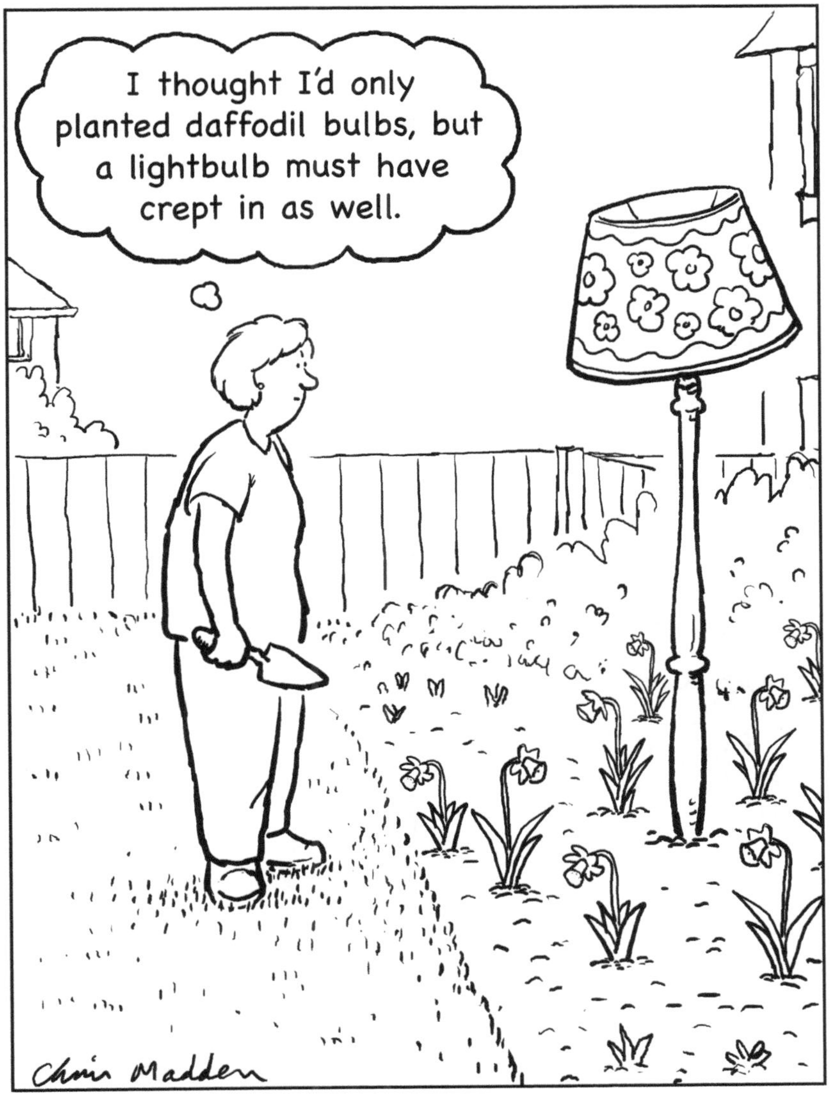
I thought I'd only planted daffodil bulbs, but a lightbulb must have crept in as well.
Chris Madden

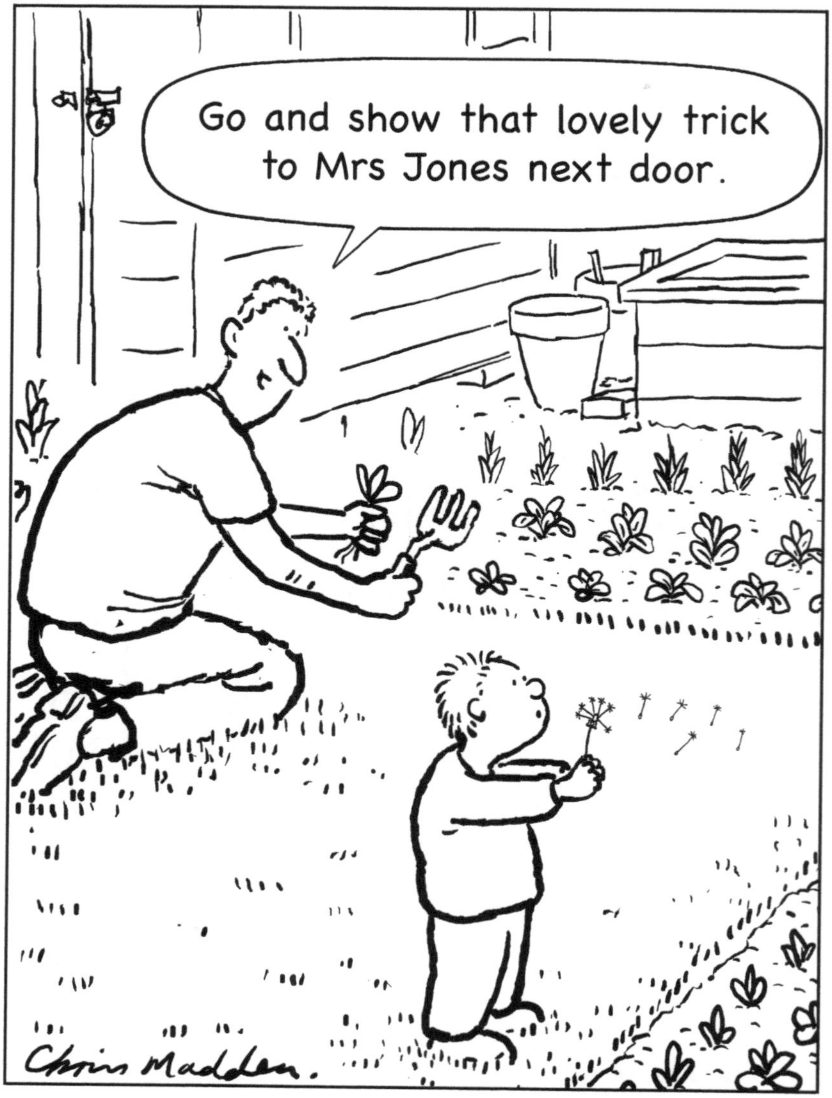
Go and show that lovely trick to Mrs Jones next door.
Chris Madden.

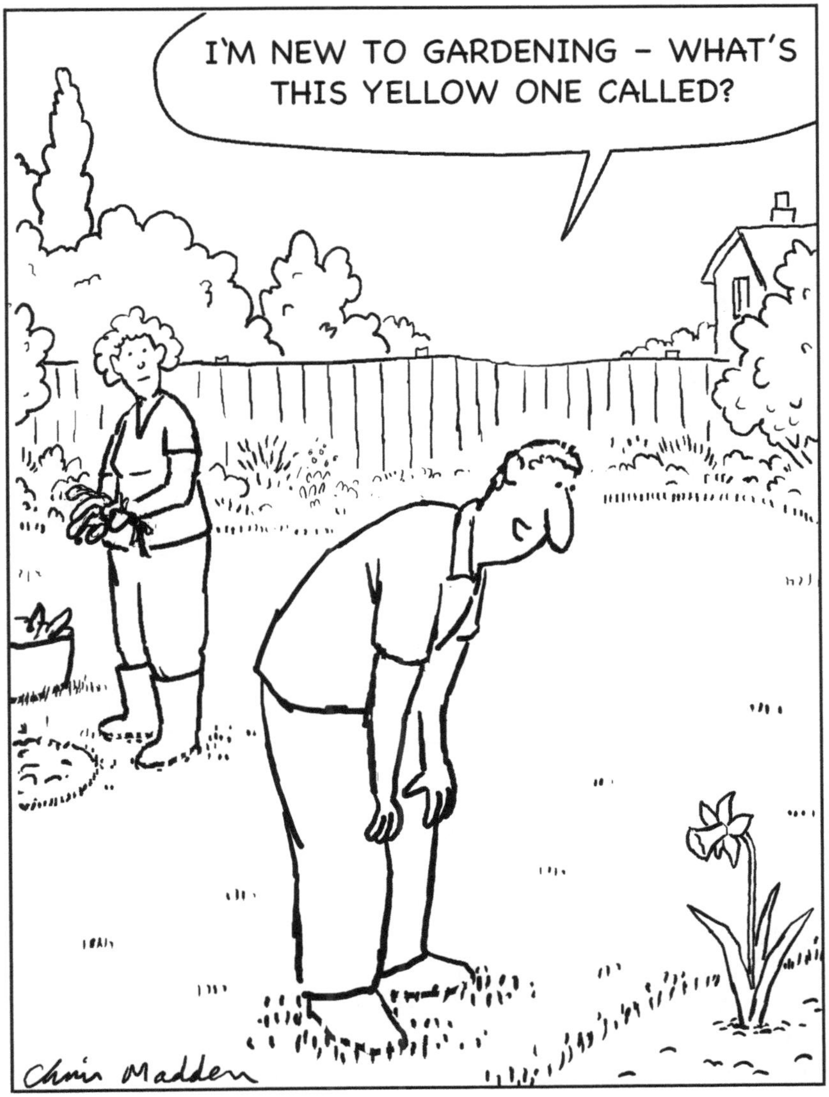
I'M NEW TO GARDENING - WHAT'S THIS YELLOW ONE CALLED?
Chris Madden

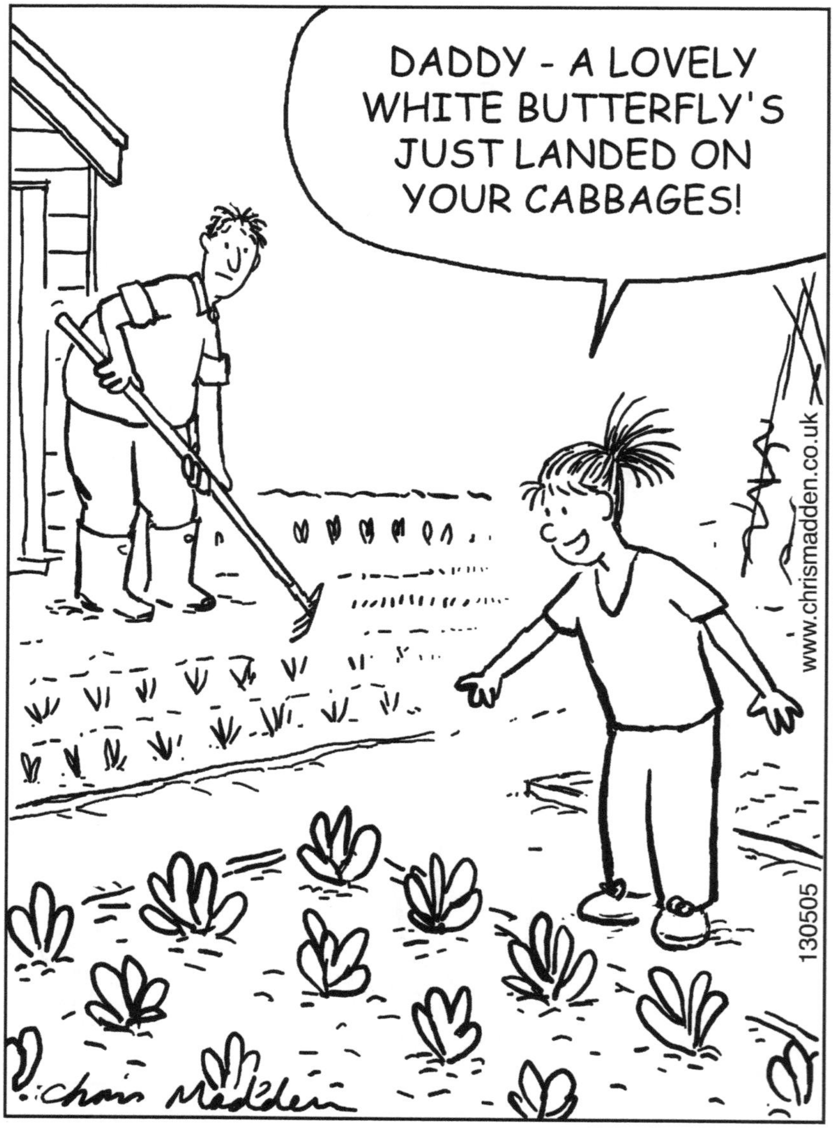
DADDY - A LOVELY WHITE BUTTERFLY'S JUST LANDED ON YOUR CABBAGES!
www.chrismadden.co.uk
130505
Chris Madden

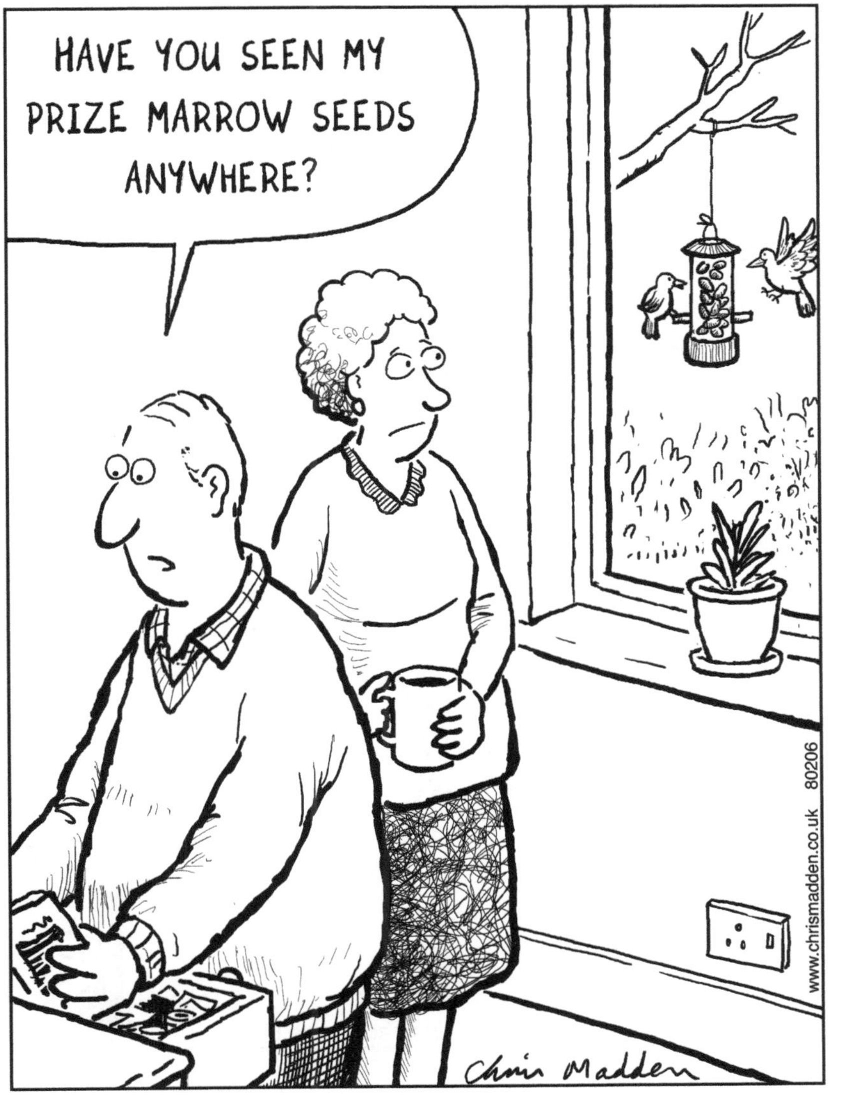
HAVE YOU SEEN MY PRIZE MARROW SEEDS ANYWHERE?
www.chrismadden.co.uk 80206
Chris Madden

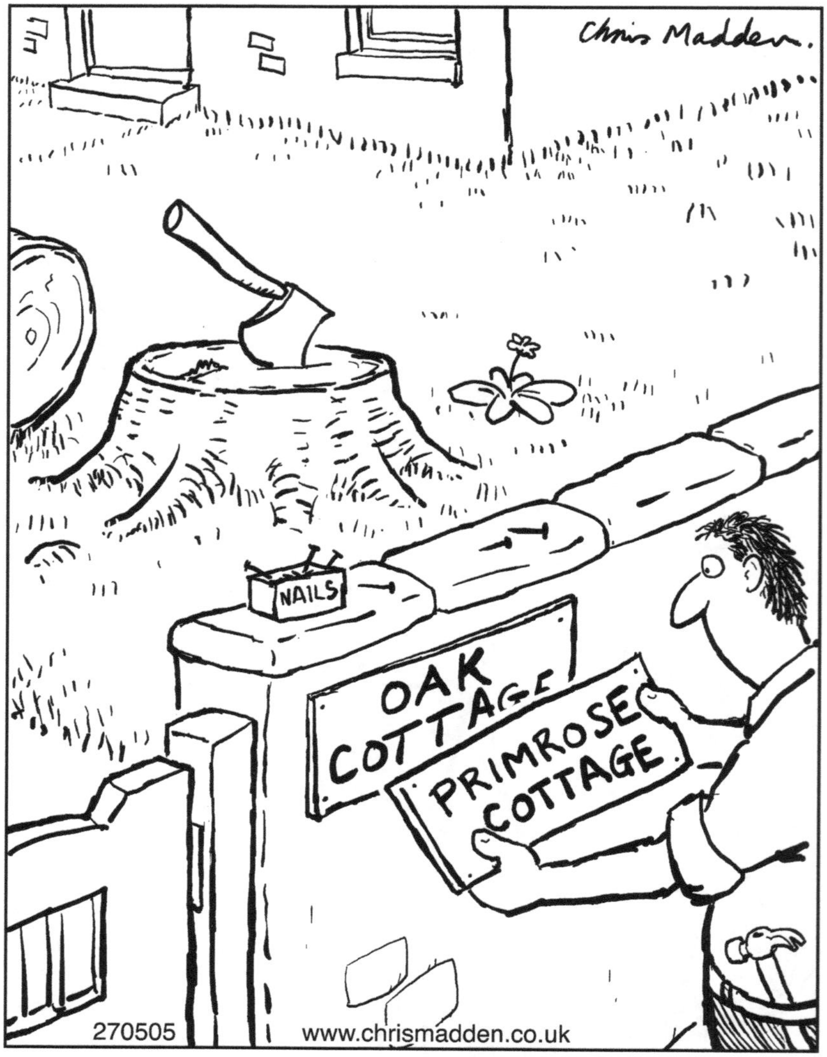
Chris Madden.
NAILS
OAK COTTAGE
PRIMROSE COTTAGE
270505
www.chrismadden.co.uk

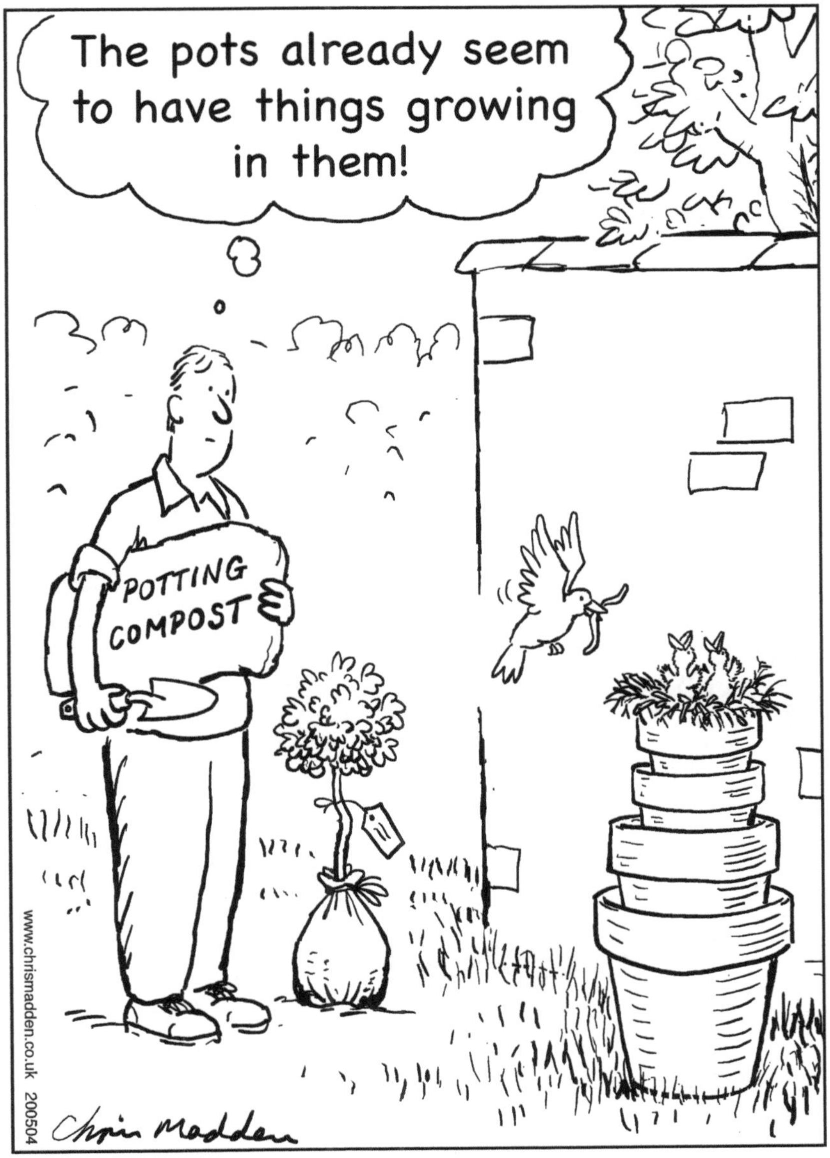
The pots already seem to have things growing in them!
POTTING COMPOST
www.chrismadden.co.uk 200504
Chris Madden

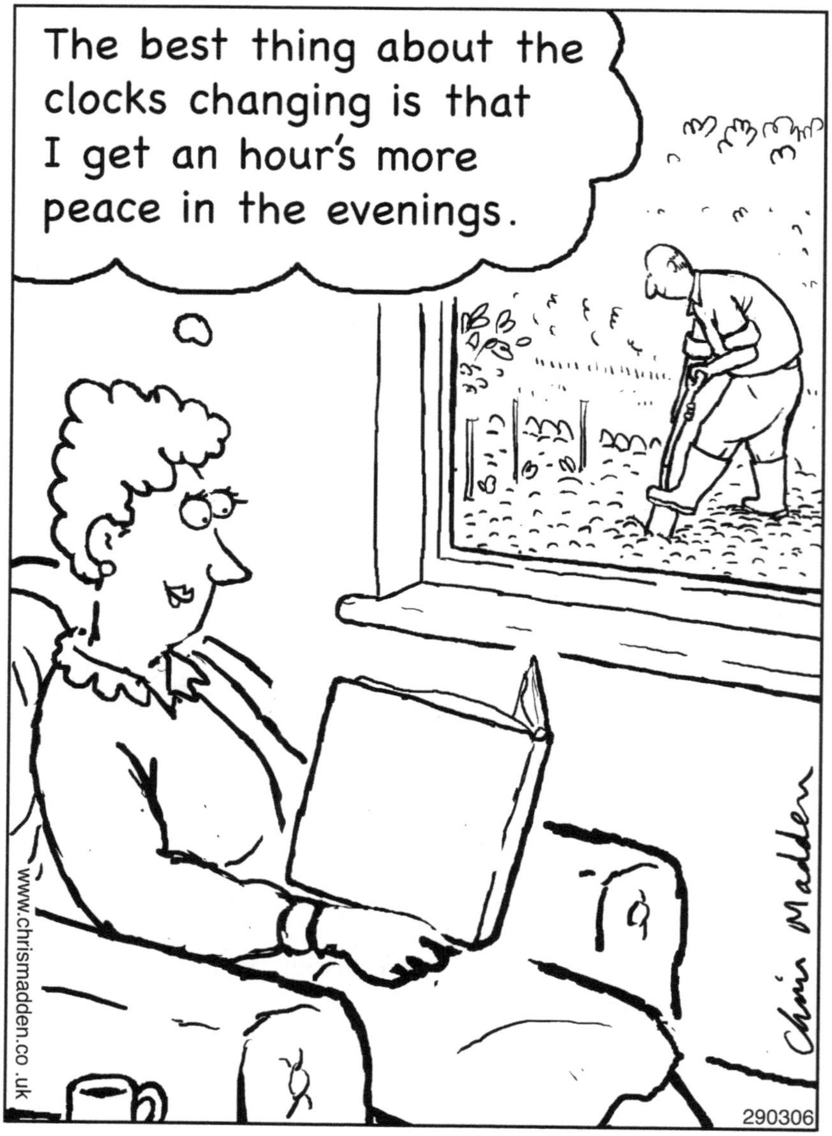
The best thing about the clocks changing is that I get an hour's more peace in the evenings.
www.chrismadden.co.uk
Chris Madden
290306

SUMMER

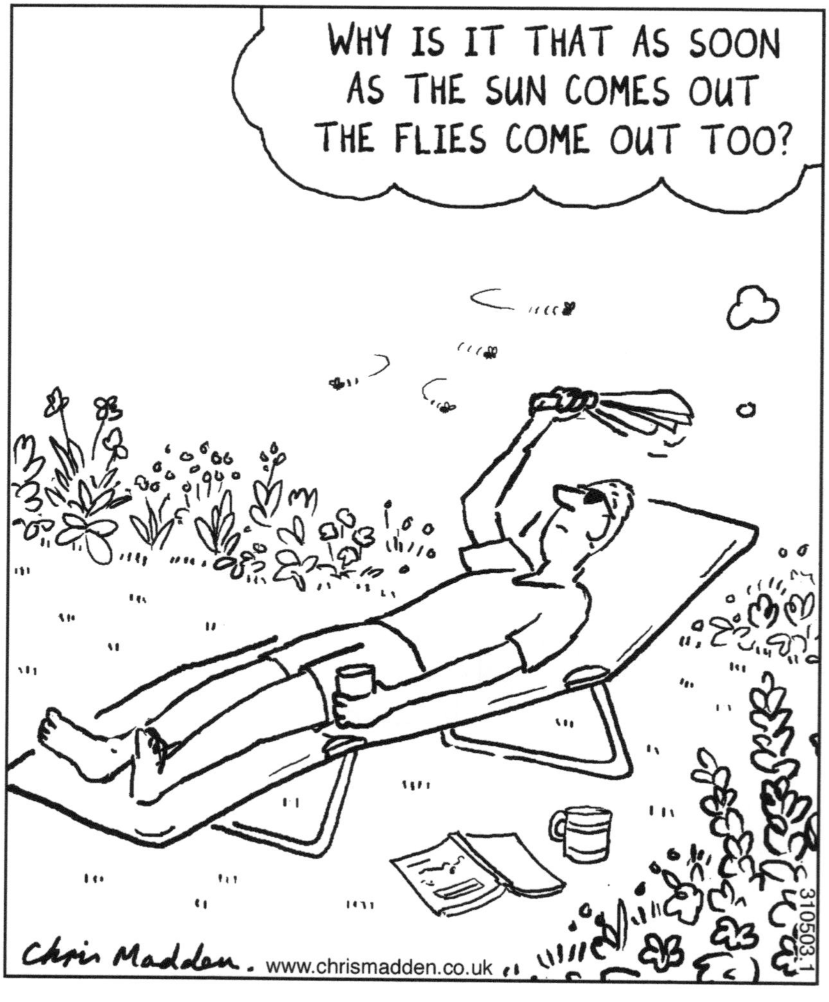
WHY IS IT THAT AS SOON AS THE SUN COMES OUT THE FLIES COME OUT TOO?
Chris Madden. www.chrismadden.co.uk
310503.1

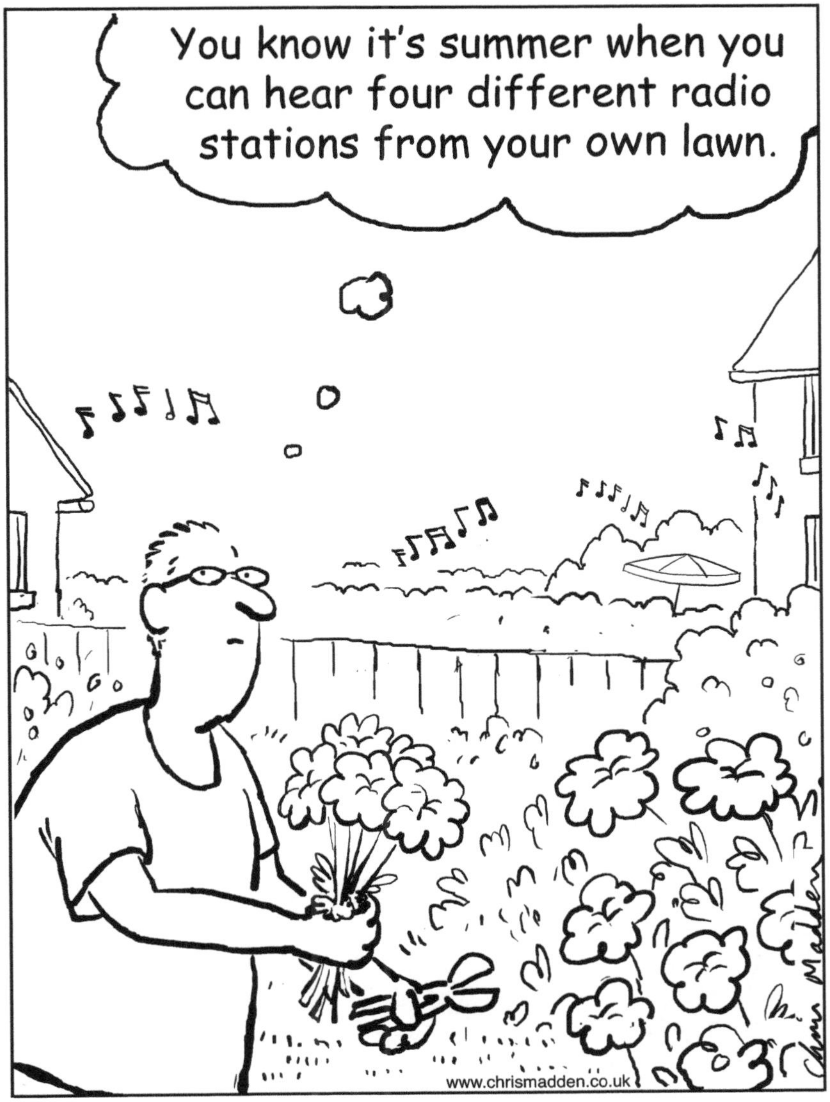
You know it's summer when you can hear four different radio stations from your own lawn.
www.chrismadden.co.uk
Chris Madden

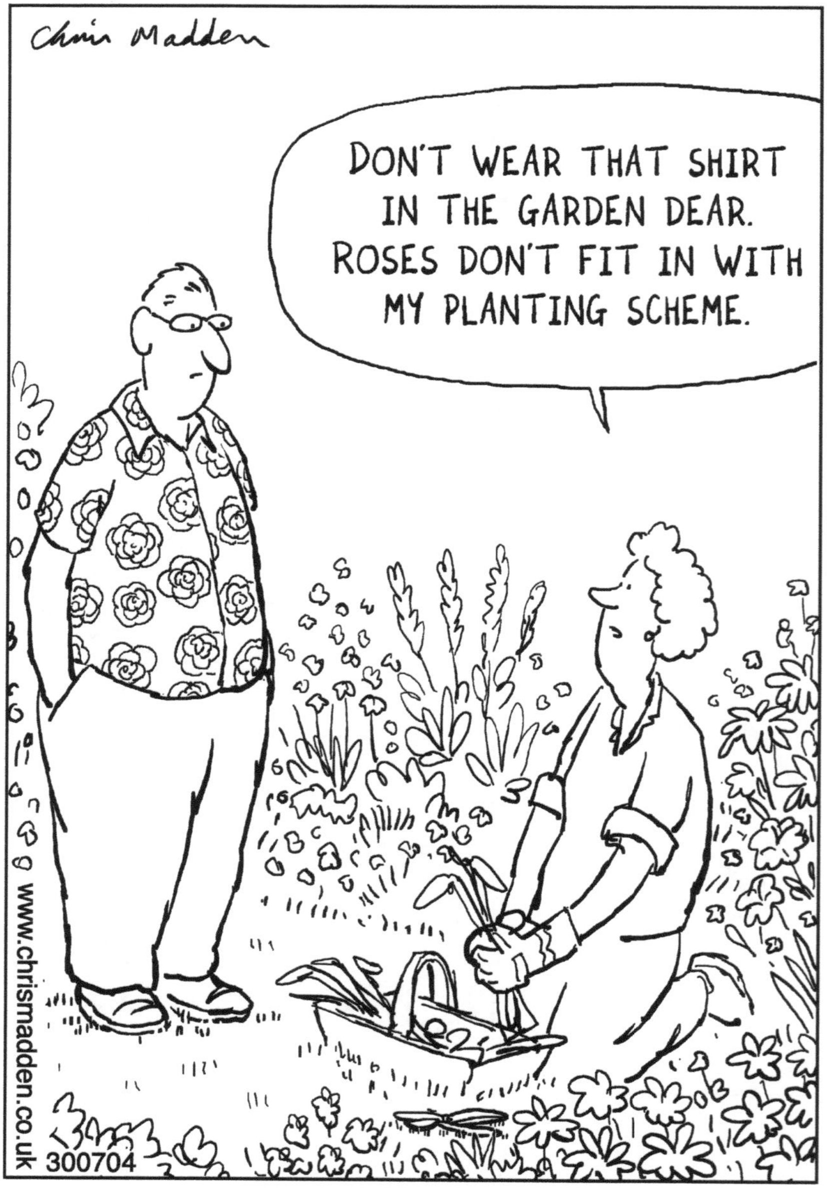
Chris Madden
DON'T WEAR THAT SHIRT IN THE GARDEN DEAR. ROSES DON'T FIT IN WITH MY PLANTING SCHEME.
www.chrismadden.co.uk
300704

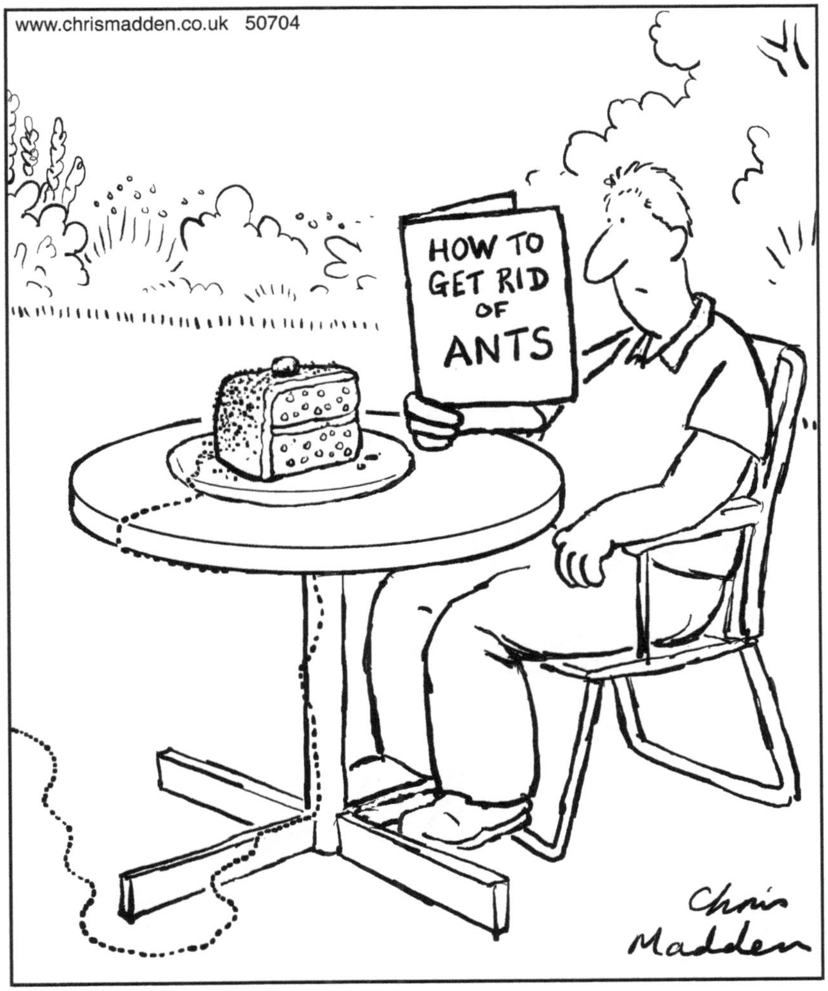
www.chrismadden.co.uk 50704
HOW TO GET RID OF ANTS
Chris Madden

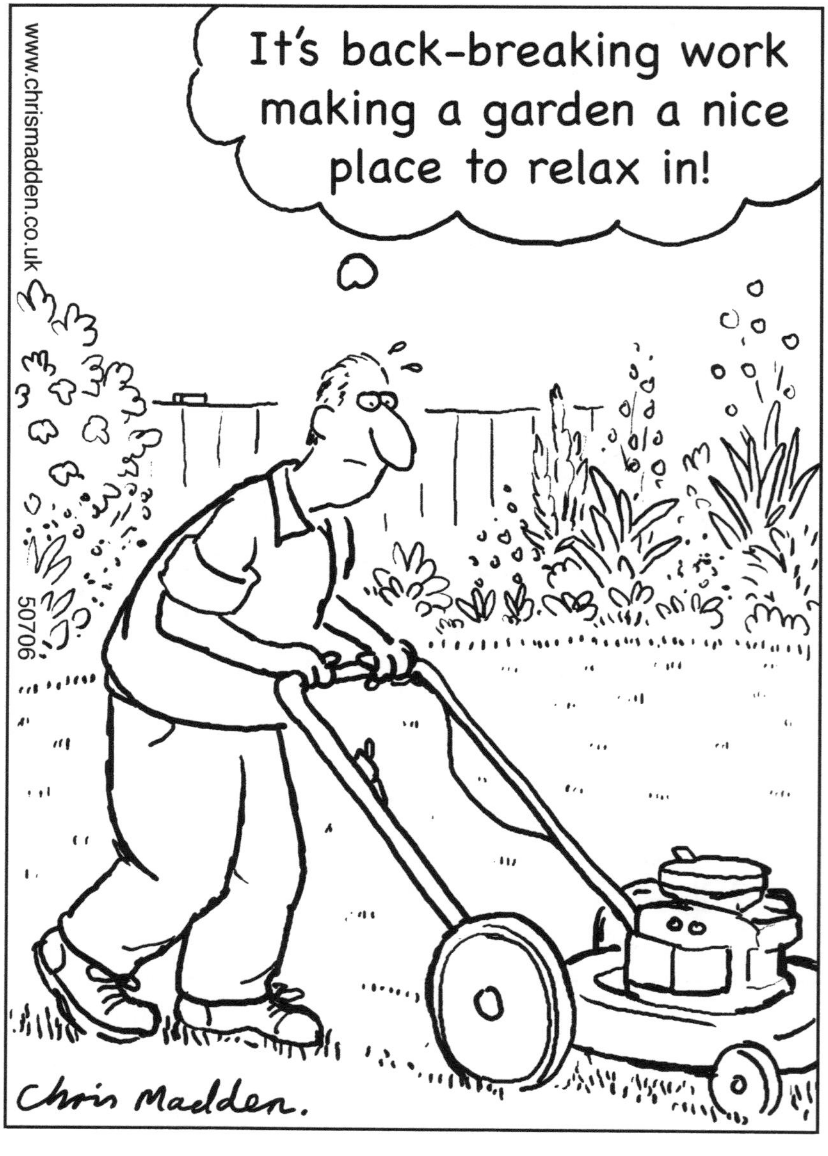
It's back-breaking work making a garden a nice place to relax in!
www.chrismadden.co.uk
50706
Chris Madden.

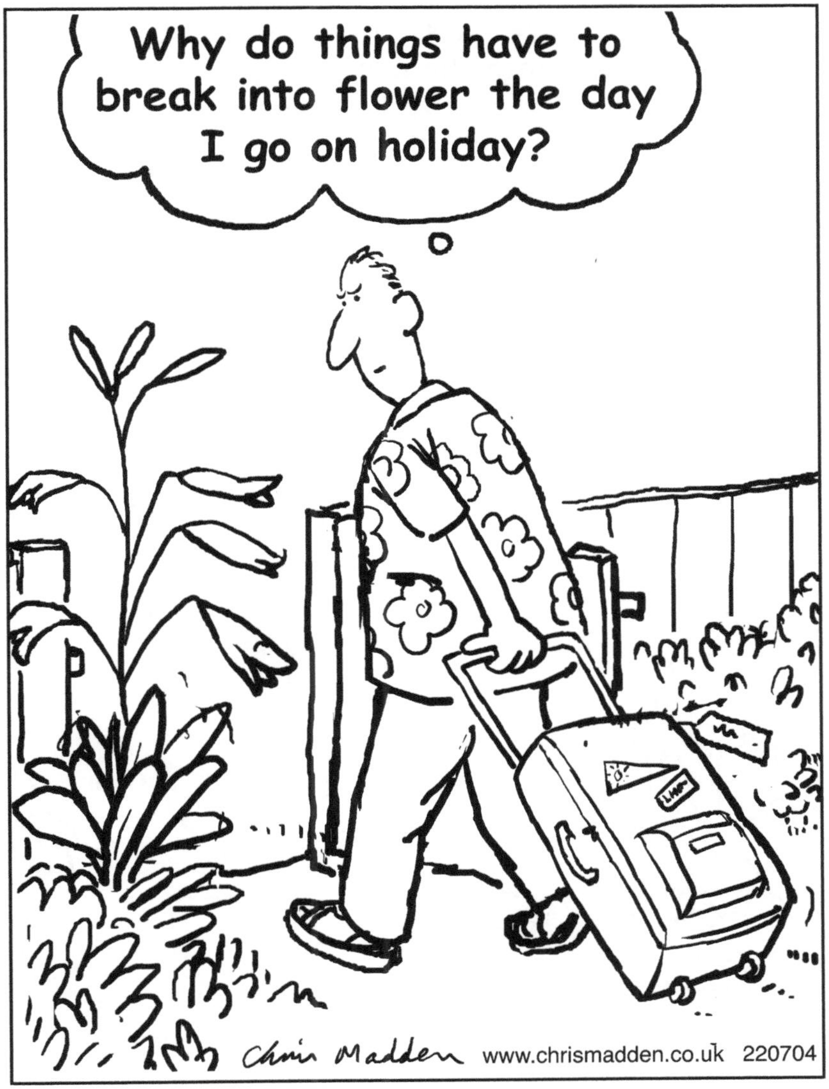
Why do things have to break into flower the day I go on holiday?
Chris Madden www.chrismadden.co.uk 220704

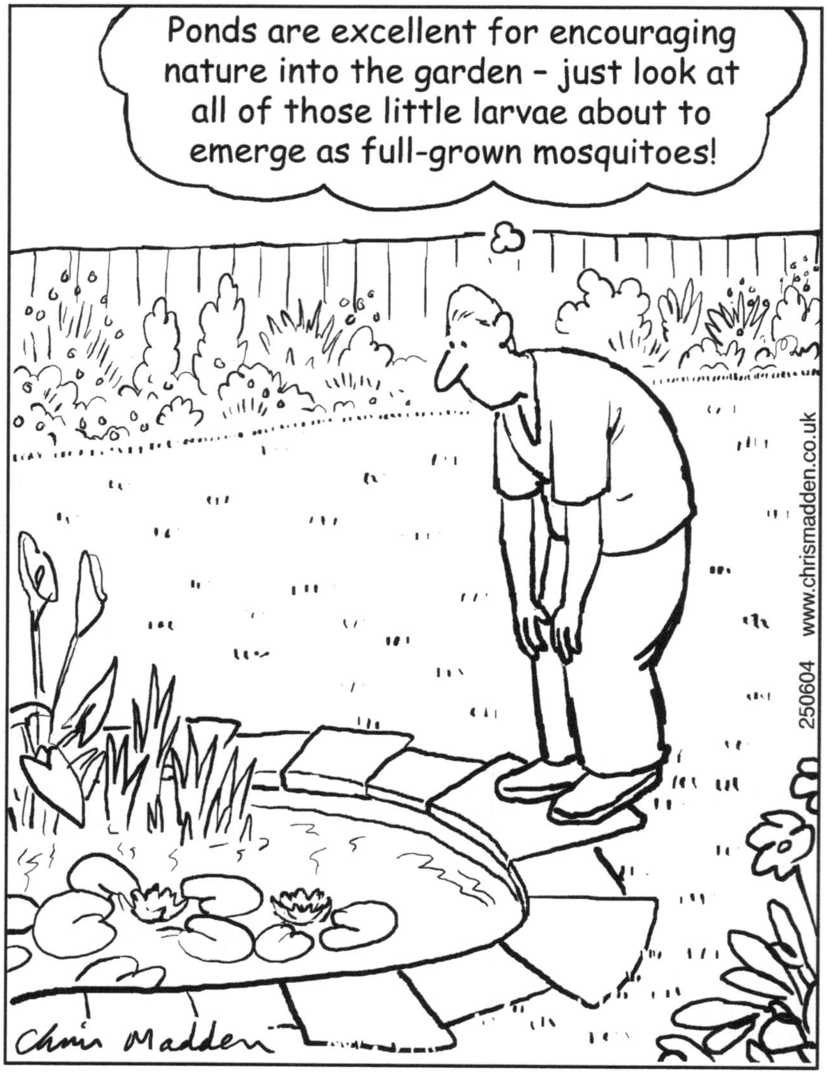
Ponds are excellent for encouraging nature into the garden - just look at all of those little larvae about to emerge as full-grown mosquitoes!
Chris Madden
250604 www.chrismadden.co.uk

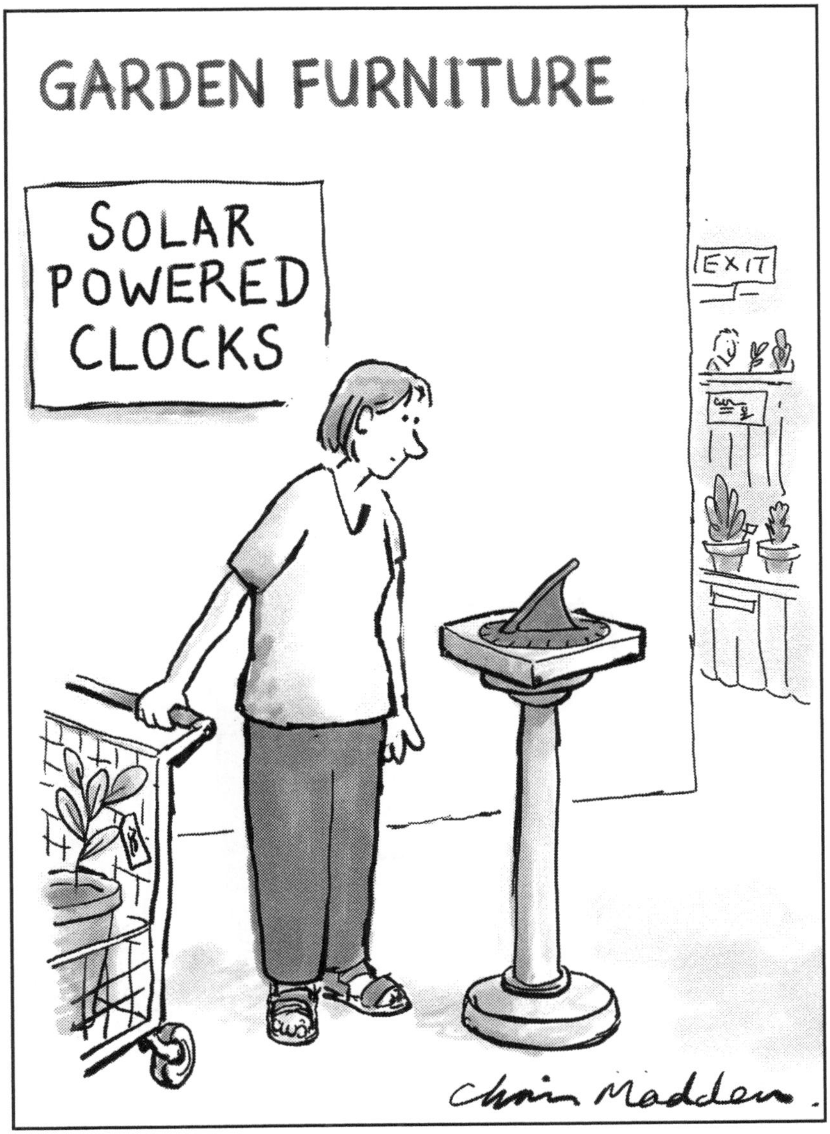
GARDEN FURNITURE
SOLAR POWERED CLOCKS
EXIT
Chris Madden

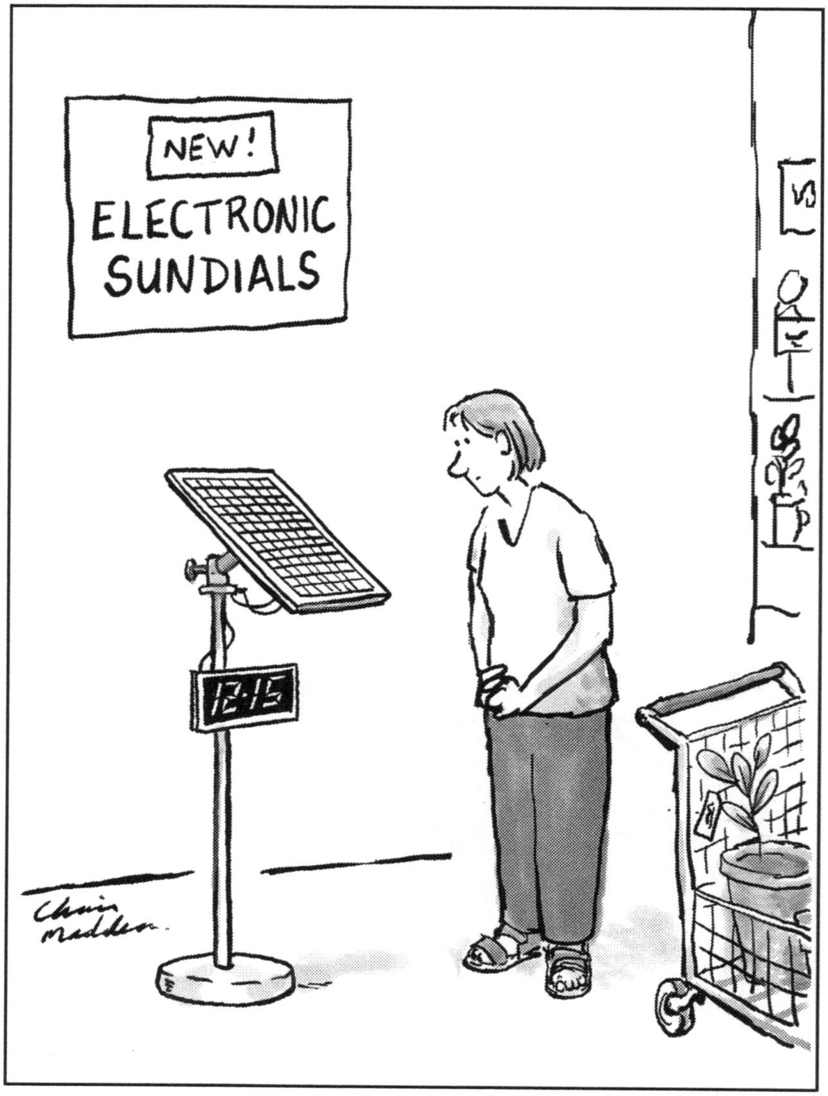
NEW!
ELECTRONIC SUNDIALS
12:15
Chris Madden

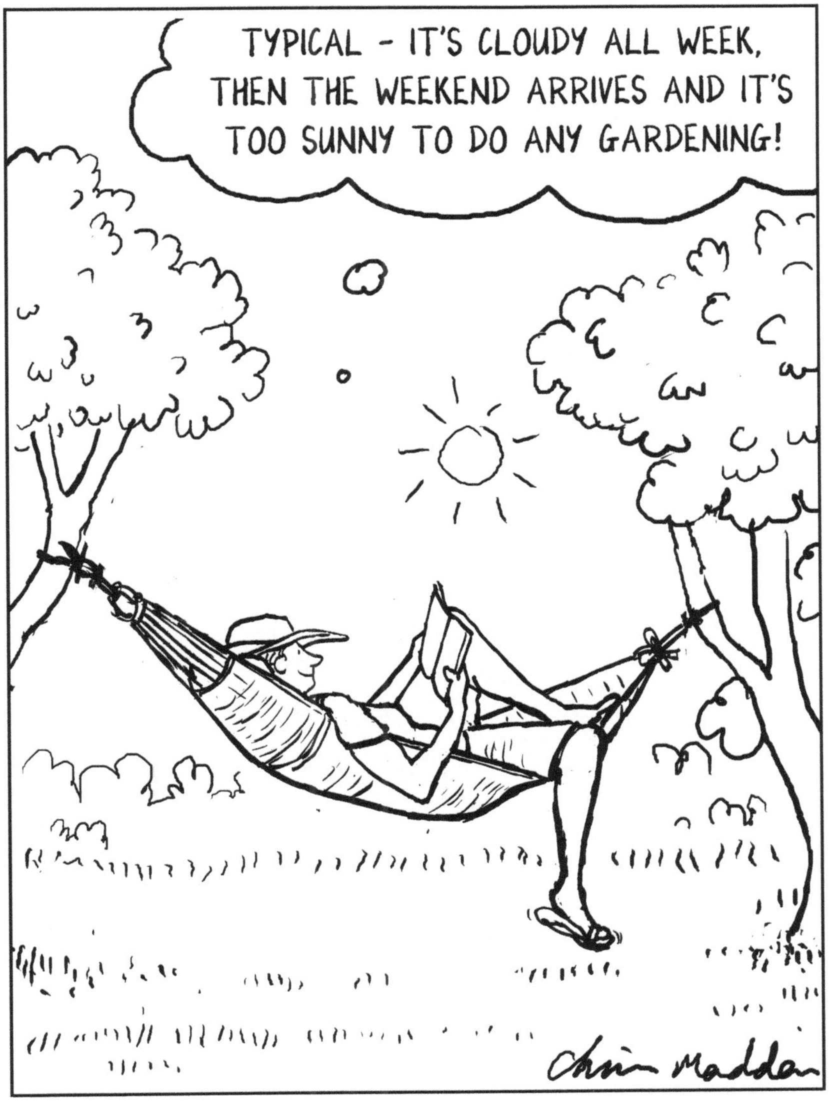
TYPICAL - IT'S CLOUDY ALL WEEK, THEN THE WEEKEND ARRIVES AND IT'S TOO SUNNY TO DO ANY GARDENING!
Chris Madden

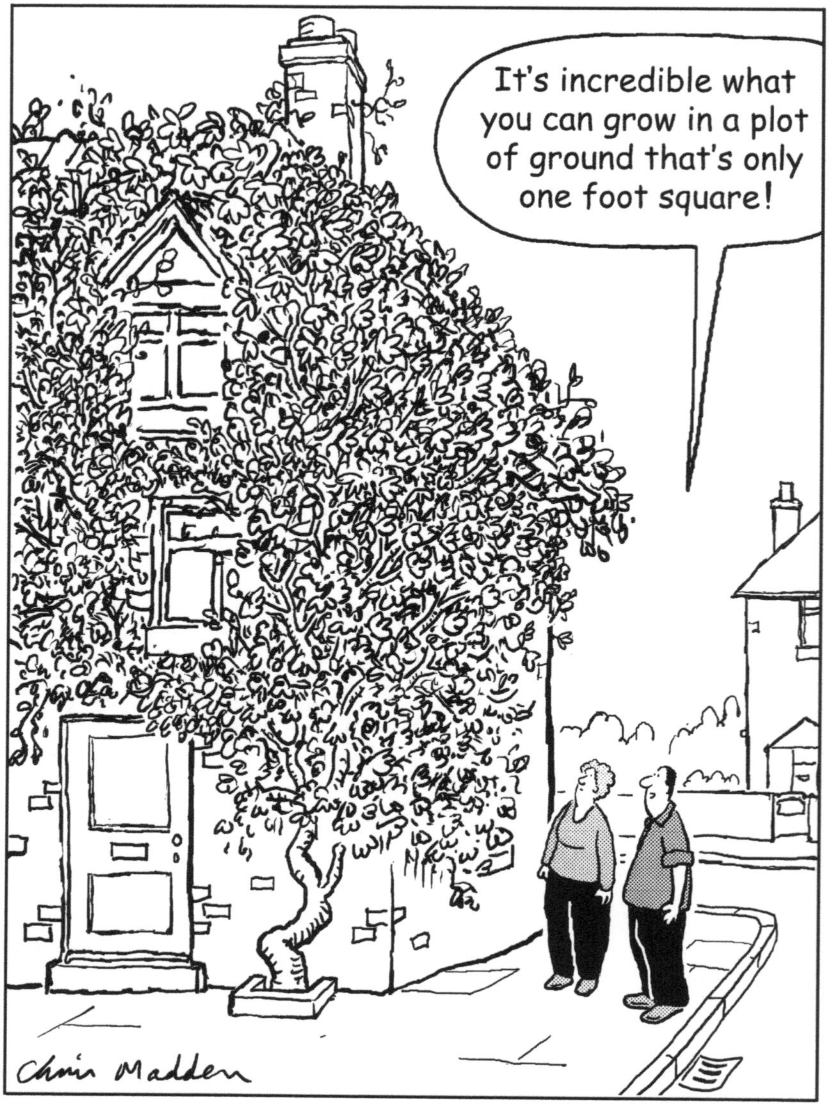
It's incredible what you can grow in a plot of ground that's only one foot square!
Chris Madden

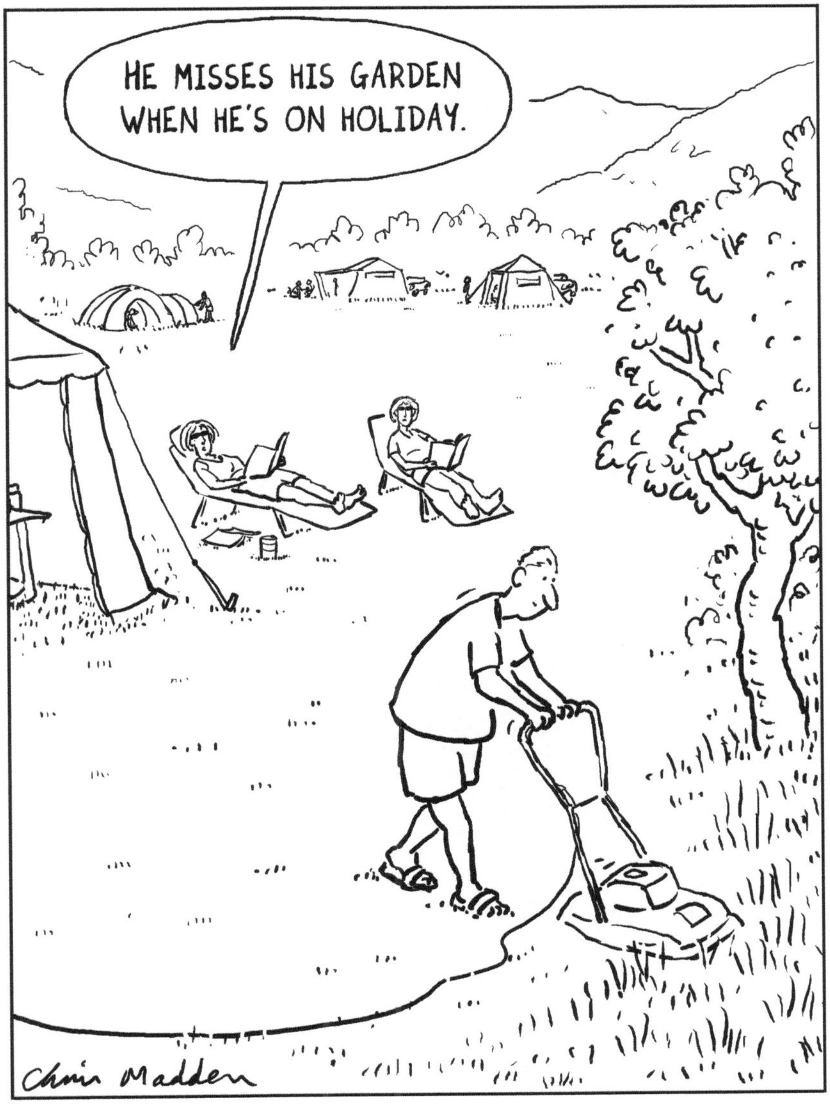
HE MISSES HIS GARDEN WHEN HE'S ON HOLIDAY.
Chris Madden

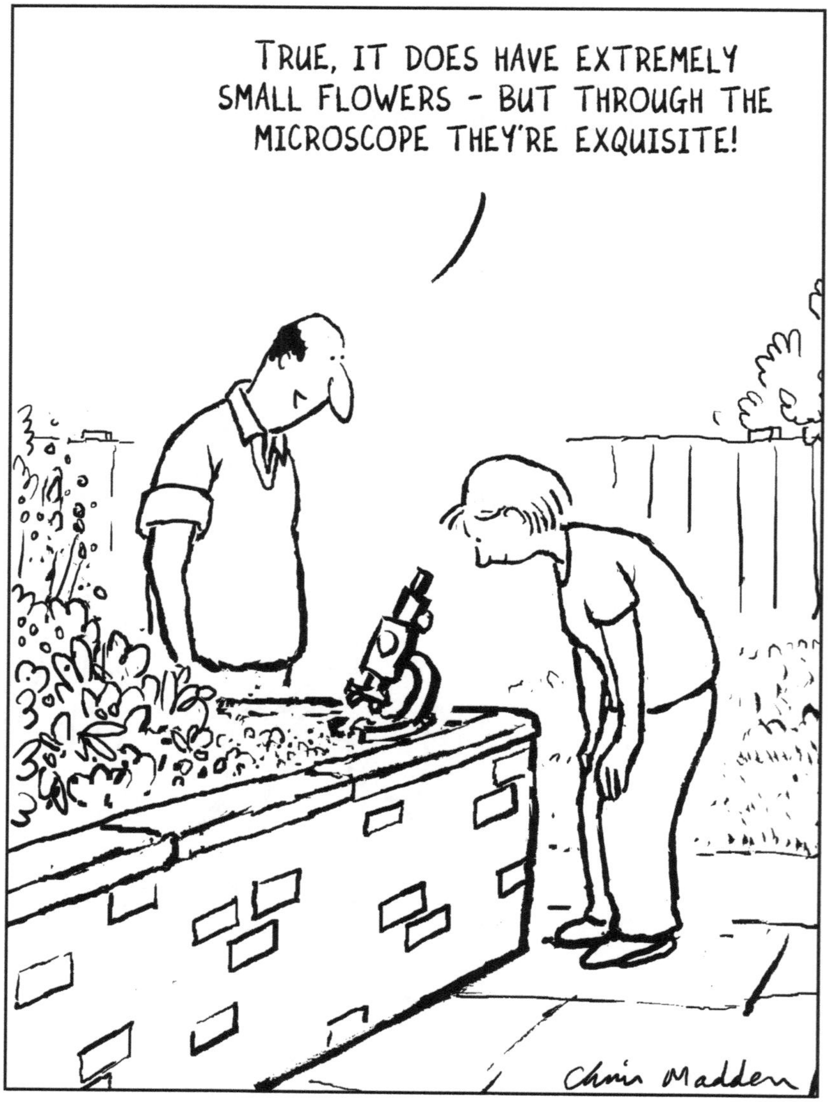
TRUE, IT DOES HAVE EXTREMELY SMALL FLOWERS - BUT THROUGH THE MICROSCOPE THEY'RE EXQUISITE!
Chris Madden

www.chrismadden.co.uk 181102.1

45

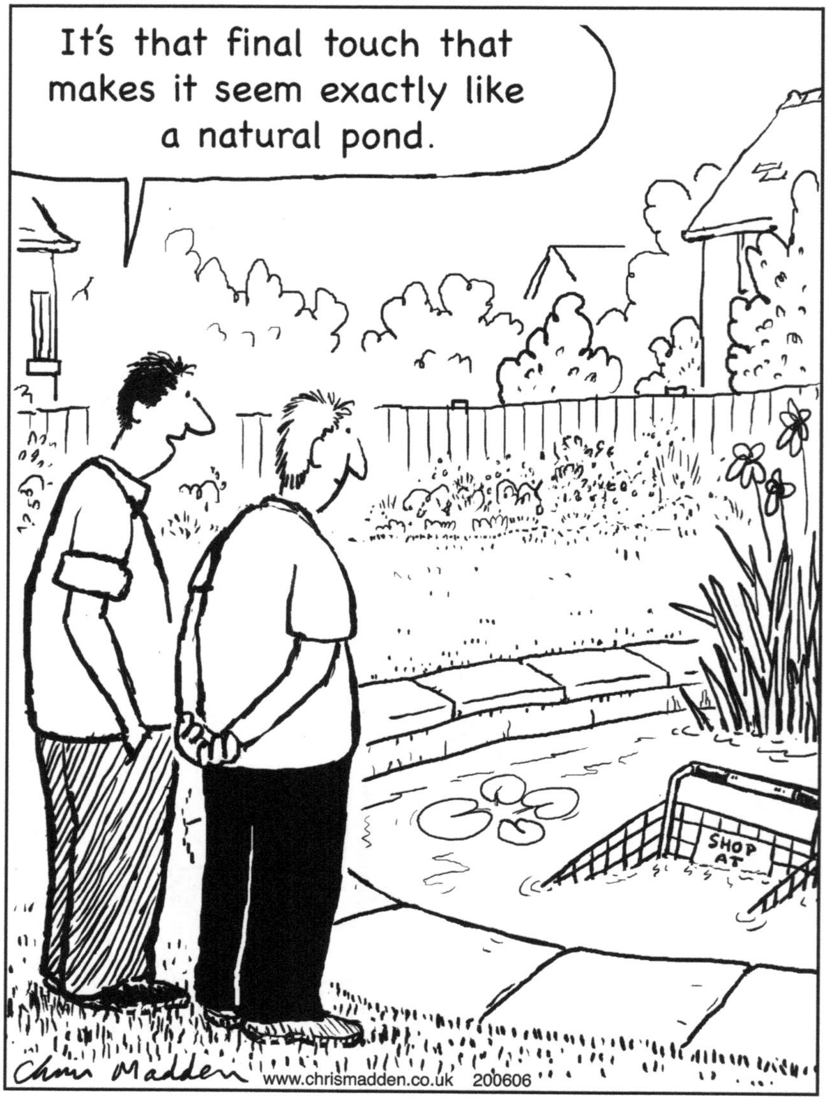
It's that final touch that makes it seem exactly like a natural pond.
SHOP AT
Chris Madden www.chrismadden.co.uk 200606

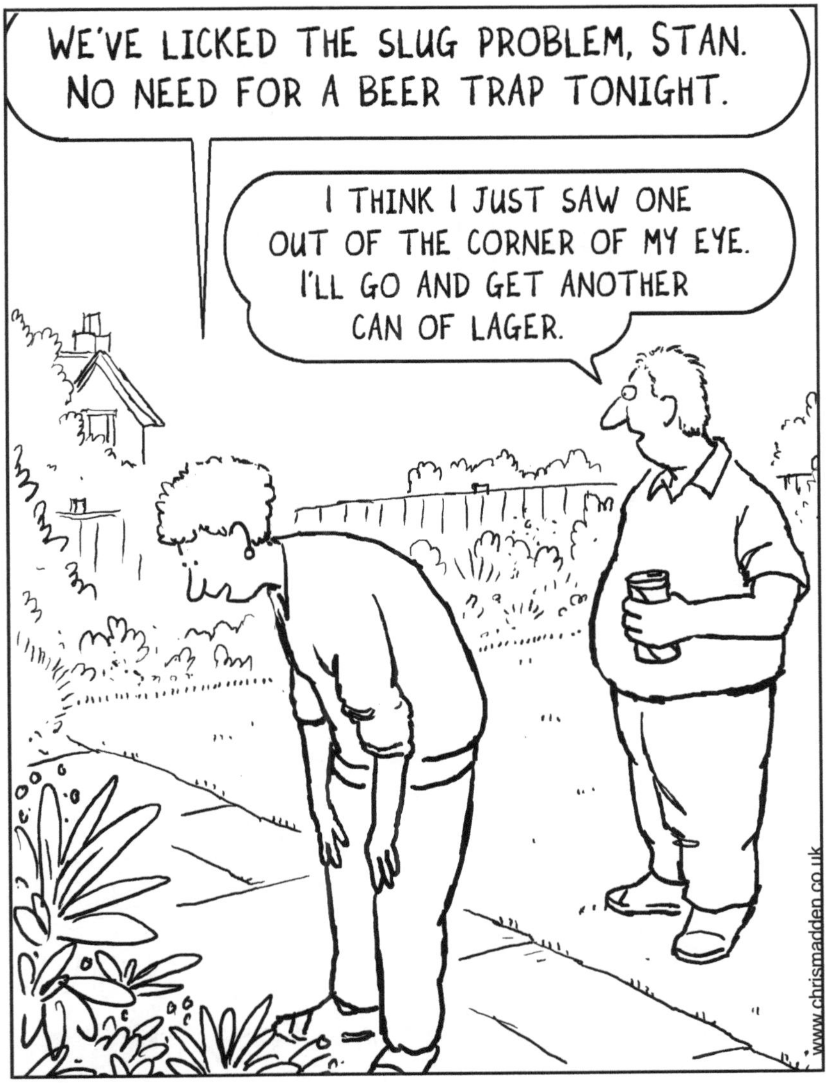
WE'VE LICKED THE SLUG PROBLEM, STAN. NO NEED FOR A BEER TRAP TONIGHT.
I THINK I JUST SAW ONE OUT OF THE CORNER OF MY EYE. I'LL GO AND GET ANOTHER CAN OF LAGER.
www.chrismadden.co.uk

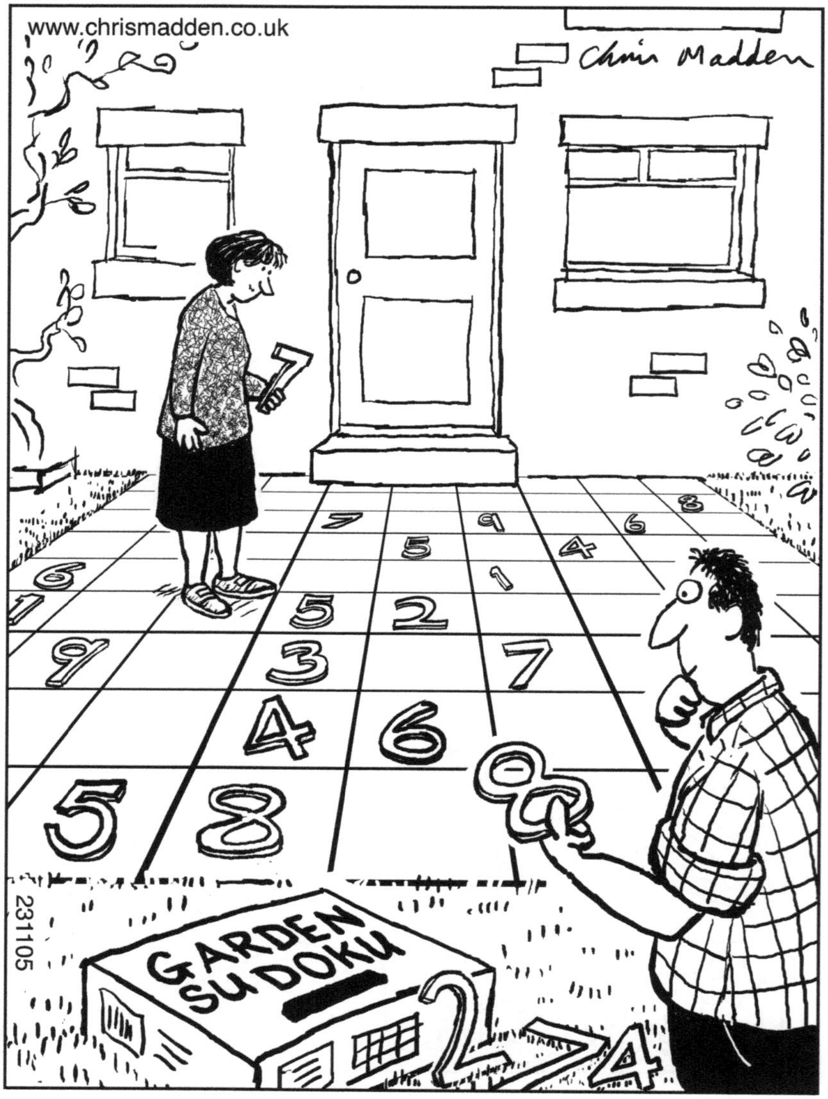
www.chrismadden.co.uk
Chris Madden
231105
GARDEN SUDOKU

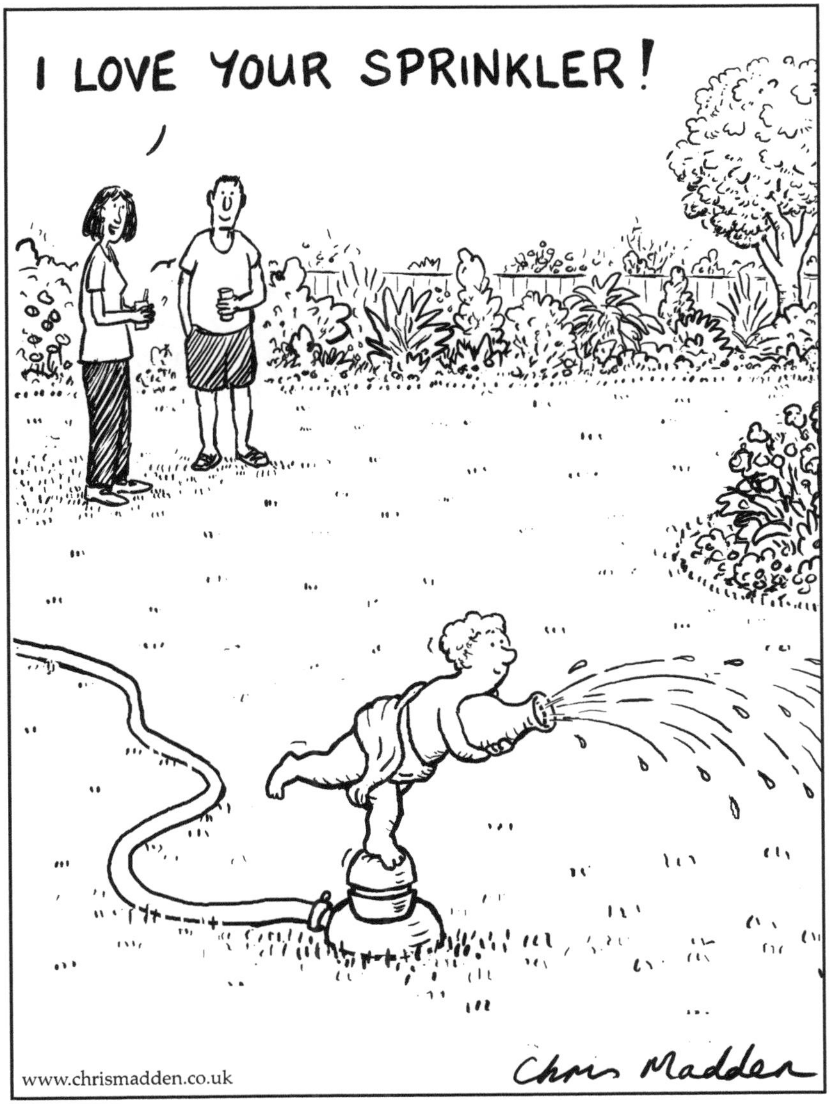
I LOVE YOUR SPRINKLER!
www.chrismadden.co.uk
Chris Madden

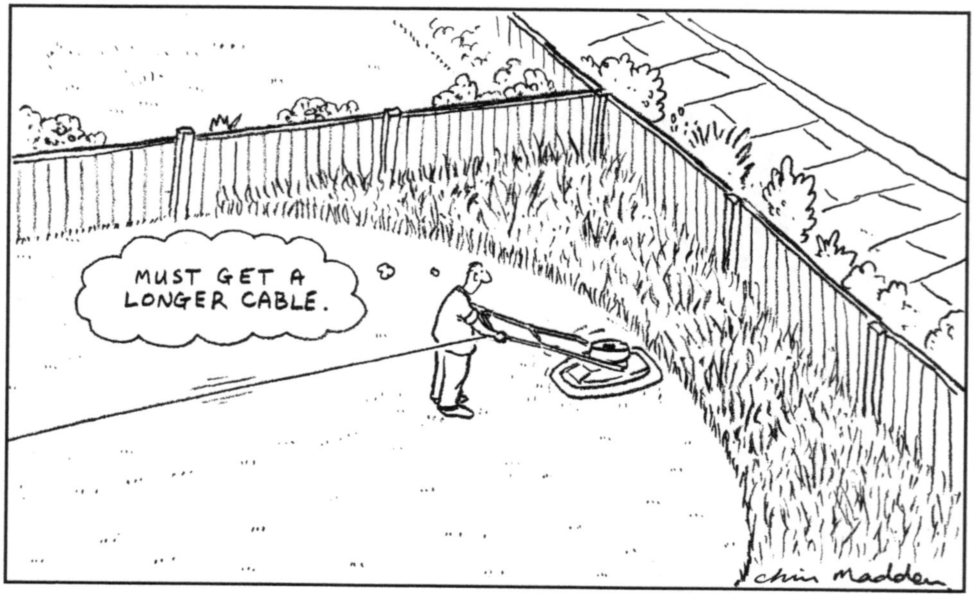
MUST GET A LONGER CABLE.
chris madden

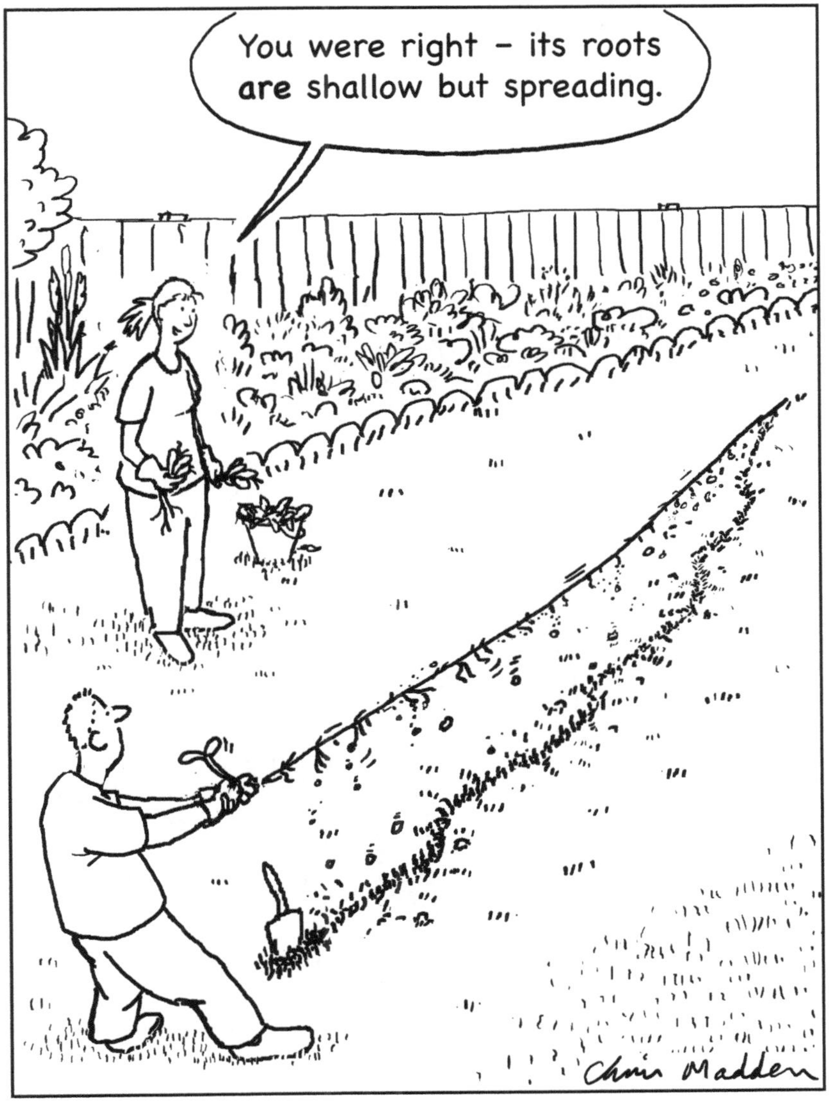
You were right - its roots are shallow but spreading.
Chris Madden

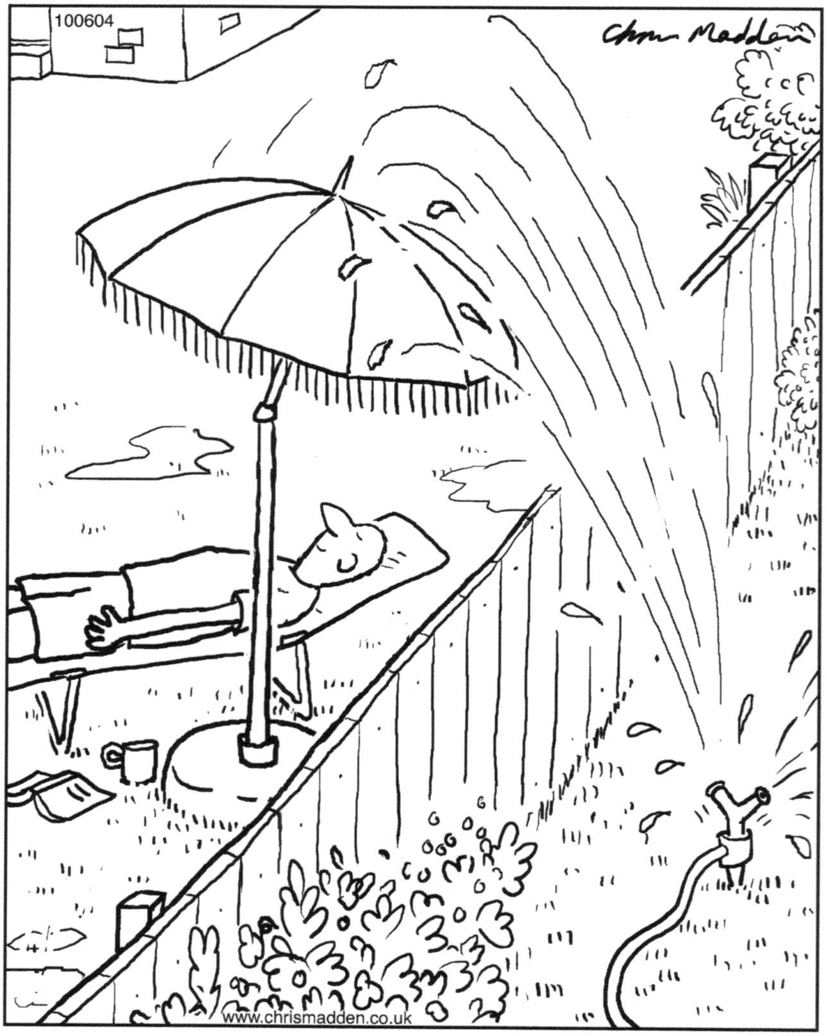
100604
Chris Madden
www.chrismadden.co.uk

GARDENING TIPS

ALLOW WORMS TO DRAG UNWANTED ORGANIC MATTER DEEP INTO THE SOIL

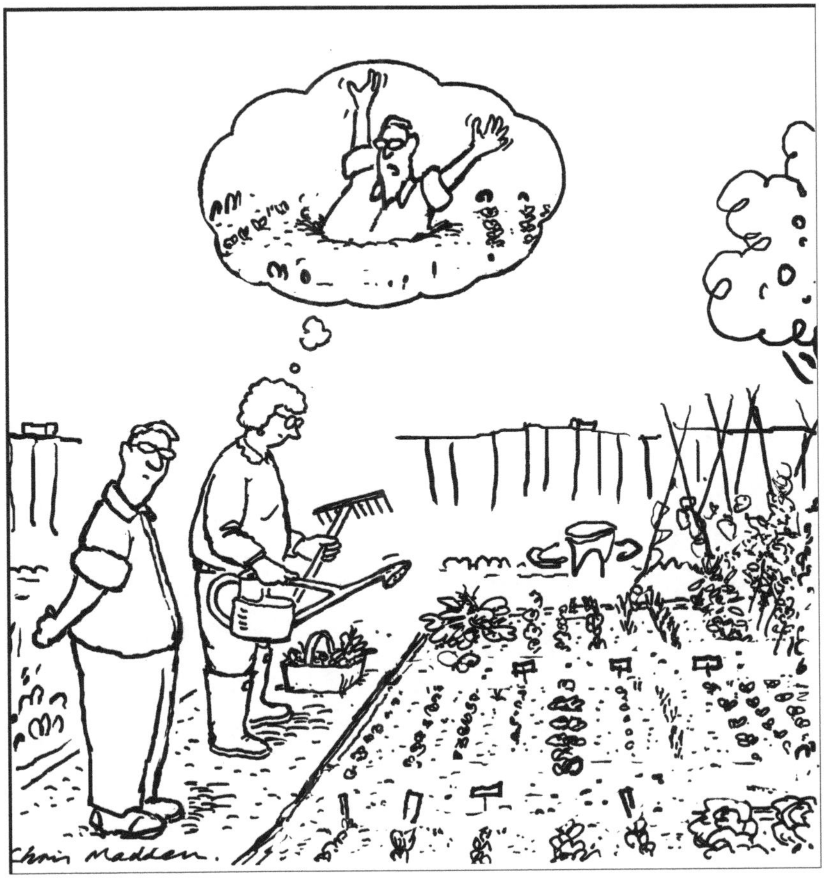
Chris Madden.

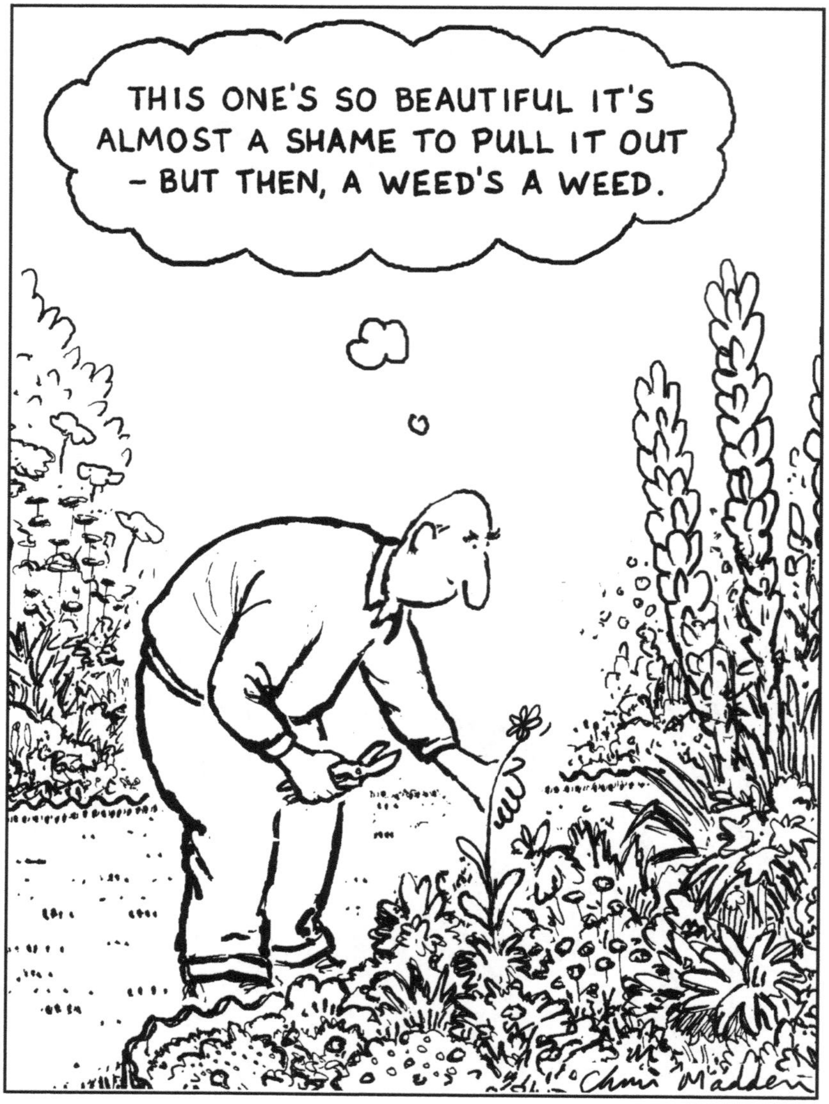
THIS ONE'S SO BEAUTIFUL IT'S ALMOST A SHAME TO PULL IT OUT – BUT THEN, A WEED'S A WEED.
Chris Madden

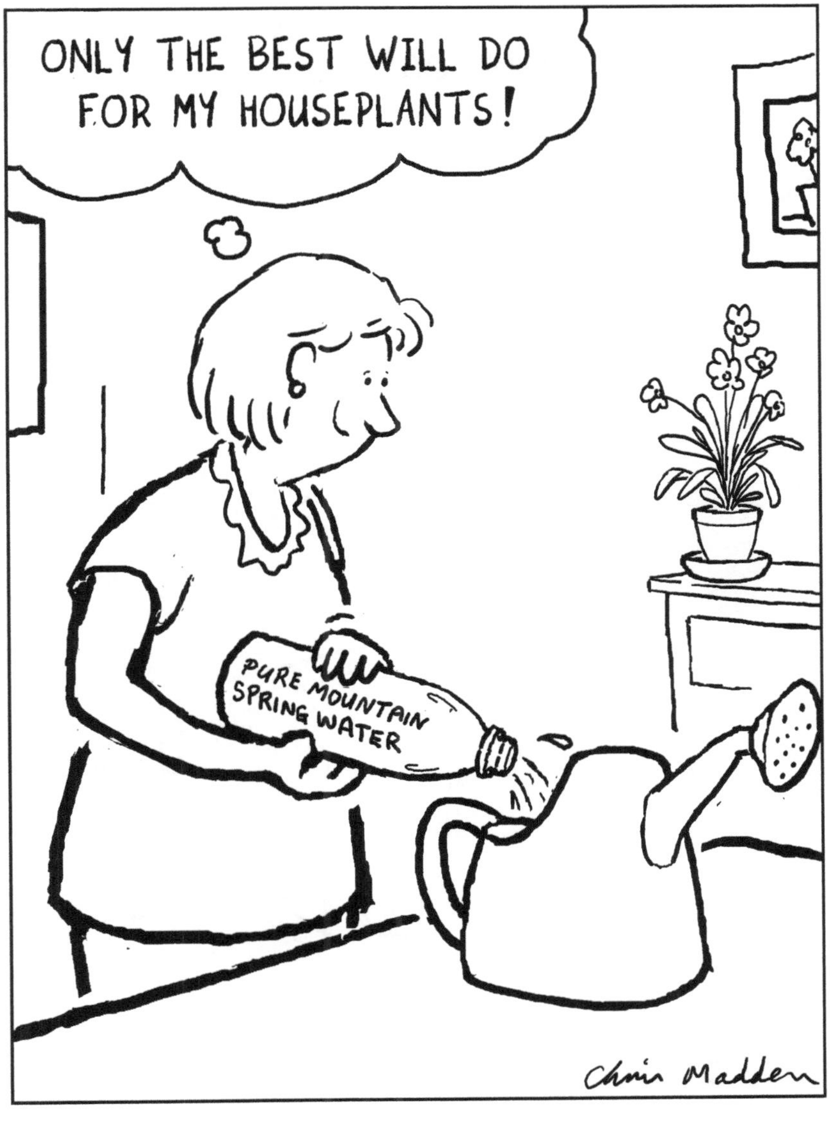
ONLY THE BEST WILL DO FOR MY HOUSEPLANTS!
PURE MOUNTAIN SPRING WATER
Chris Madden

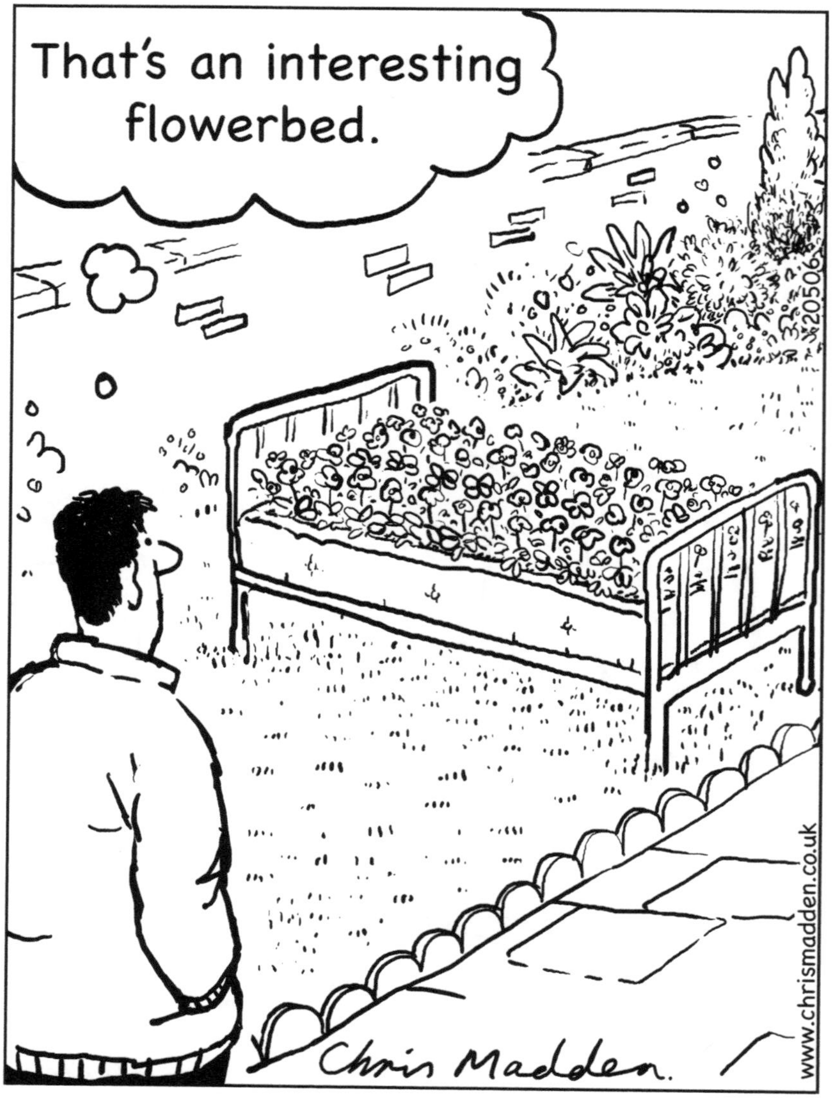
That's an interesting flowerbed.
Chris Madden.
www.chrismadden.co.uk

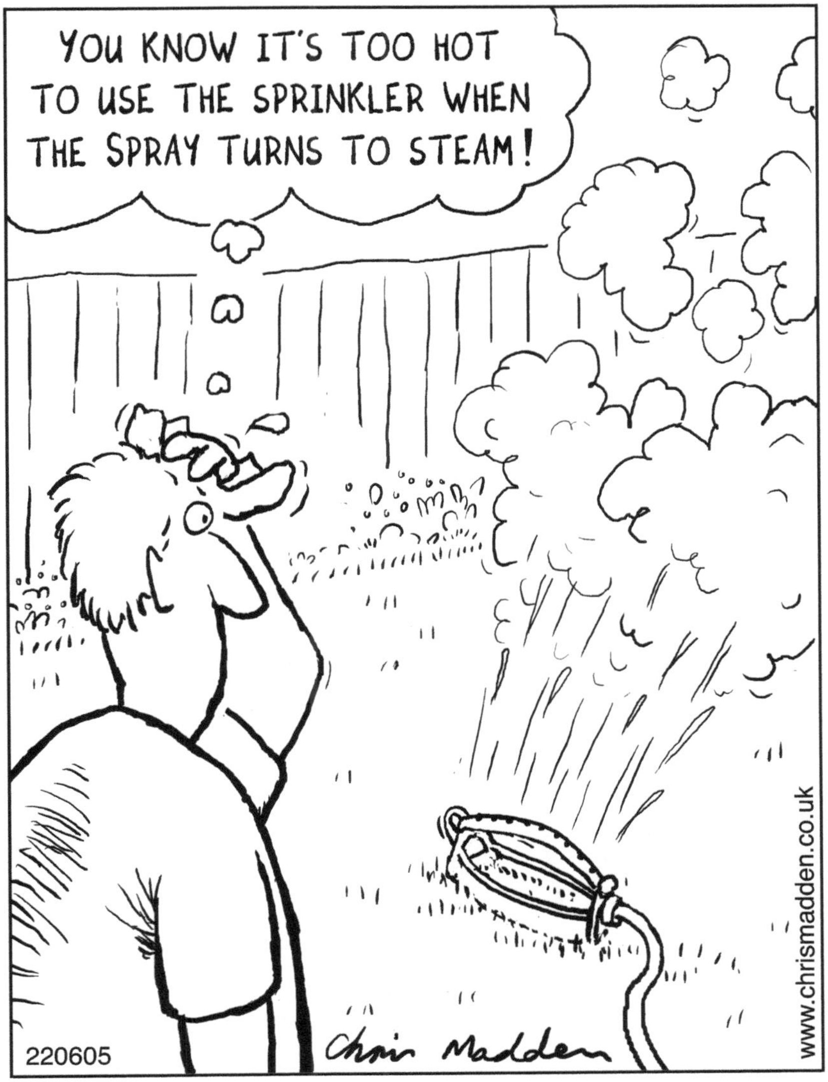
YOU KNOW IT'S TOO HOT TO USE THE SPRINKLER WHEN THE SPRAY TURNS TO STEAM!
220605
Chris Madden
www.chrismadden.co.uk

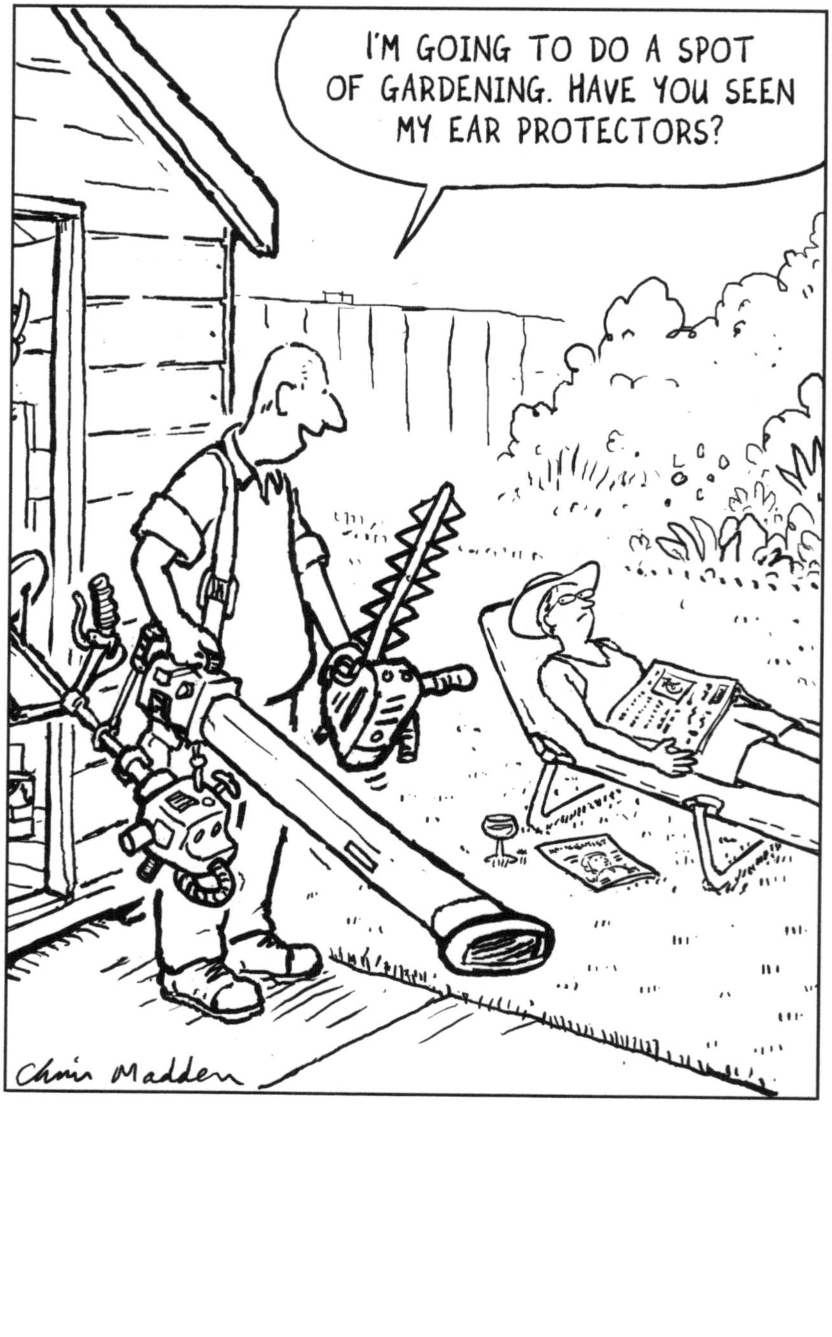
I'M GOING TO DO A SPOT OF GARDENING. HAVE YOU SEEN MY EAR PROTECTORS?
Chris Madden

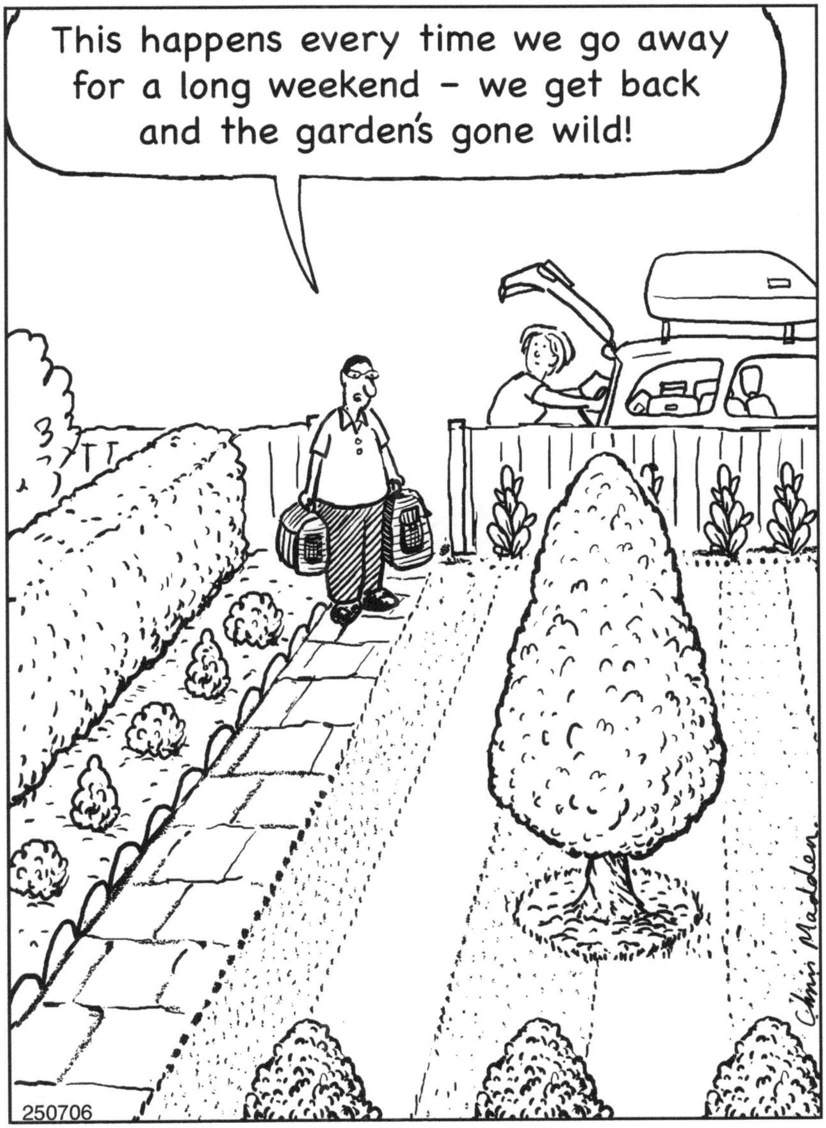
This happens every time we go away for a long weekend - we get back and the garden's gone wild!
250706

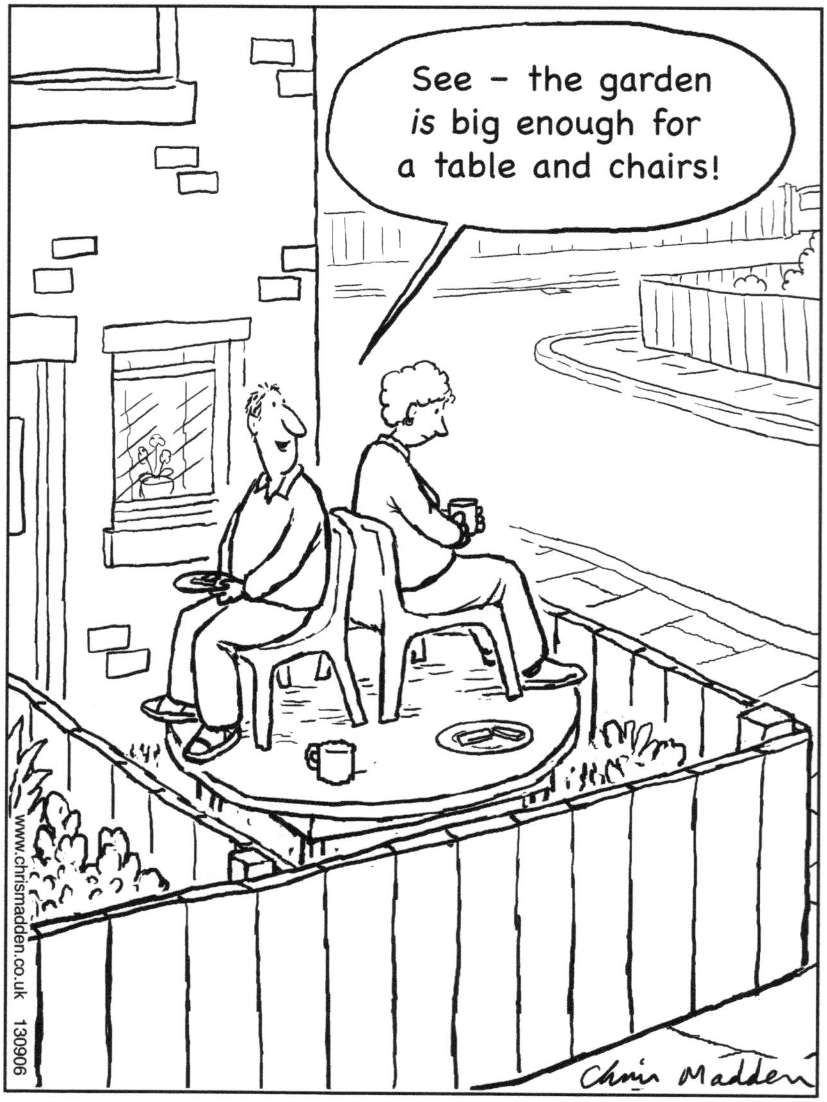
See – the garden *is* big enough for a table and chairs!
www.chrismadden.co.uk 130906
Chris Madden

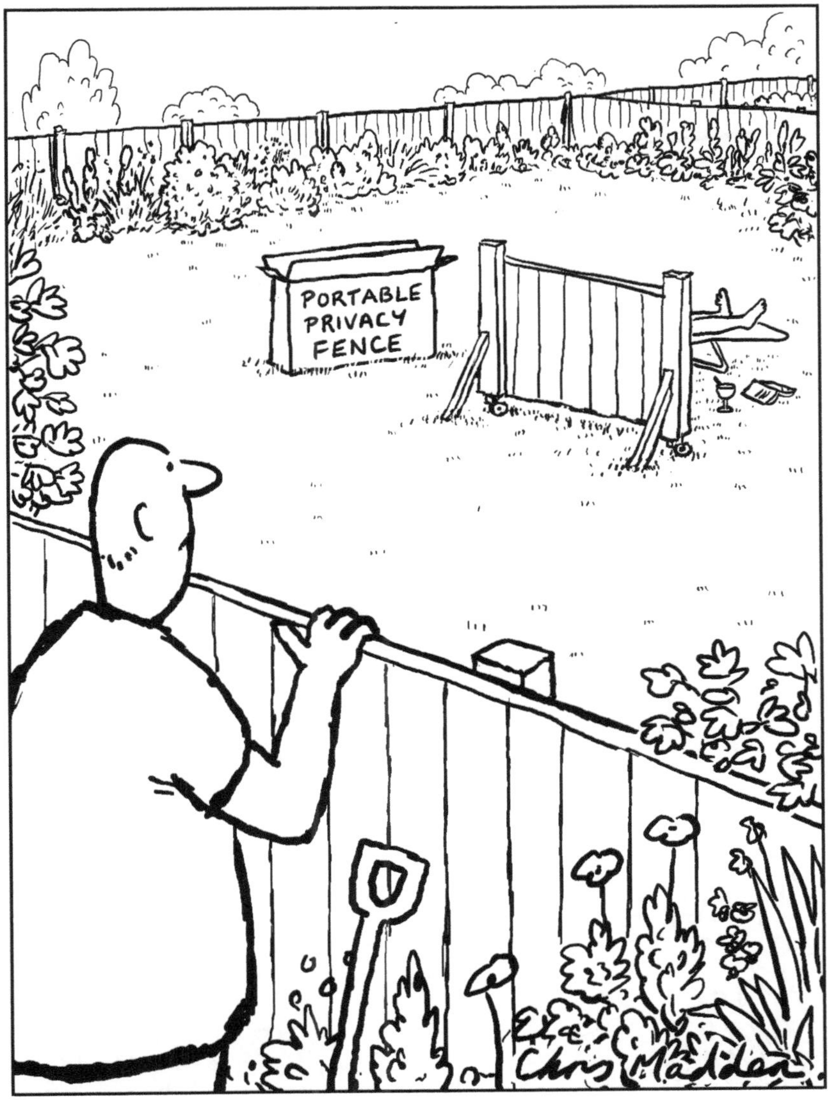
PORTABLE
PRIVACY
FENCE
Chris Madden

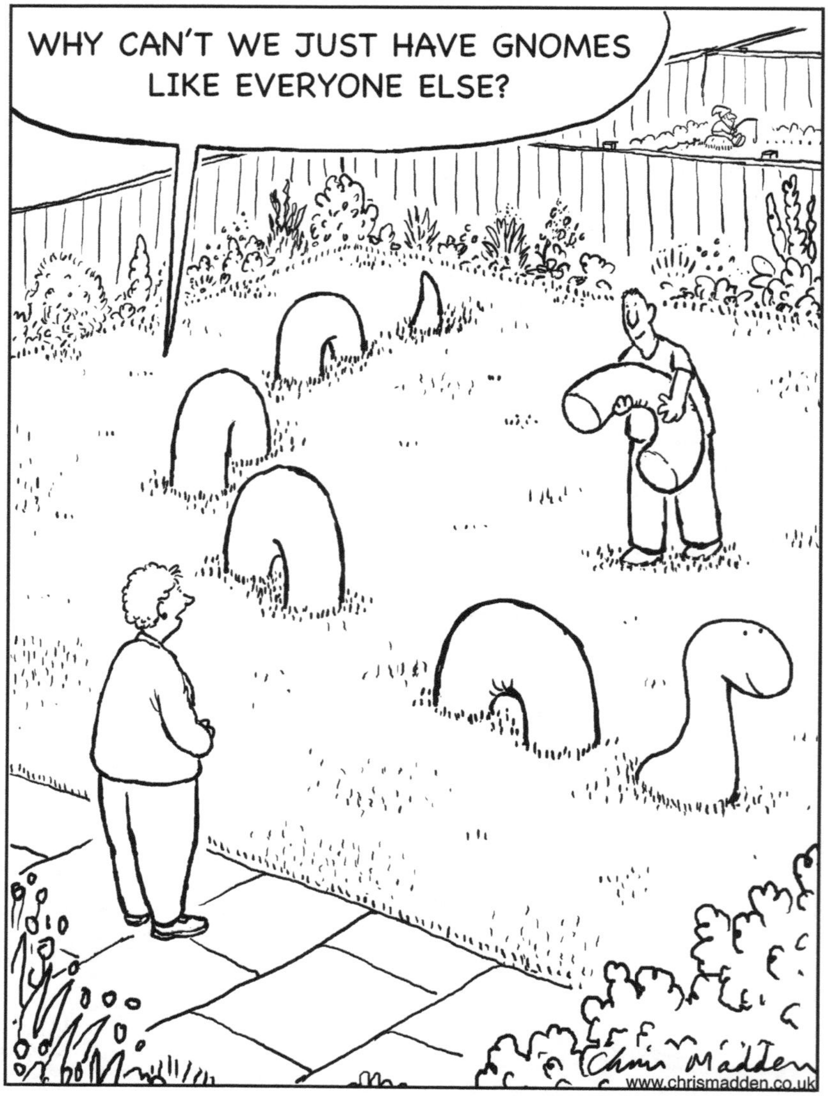
WHY CAN'T WE JUST HAVE GNOMES LIKE EVERYONE ELSE?
Chris Madden
www.chrismadden.co.uk

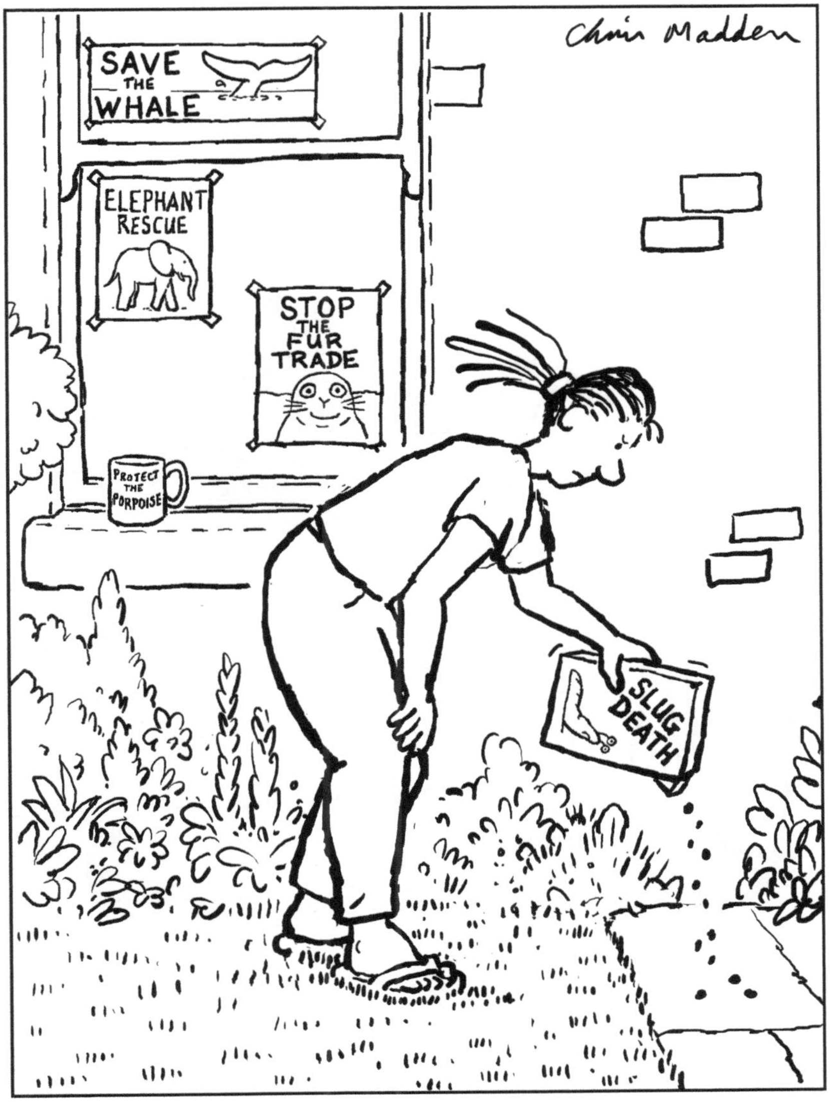
Chris Madden
SAVE
THE
WHALE
ELEPHANT
RESCUE
STOP
THE
FUR
TRADE
PROTECT
THE
PORPOISE
SLUG
DEATH

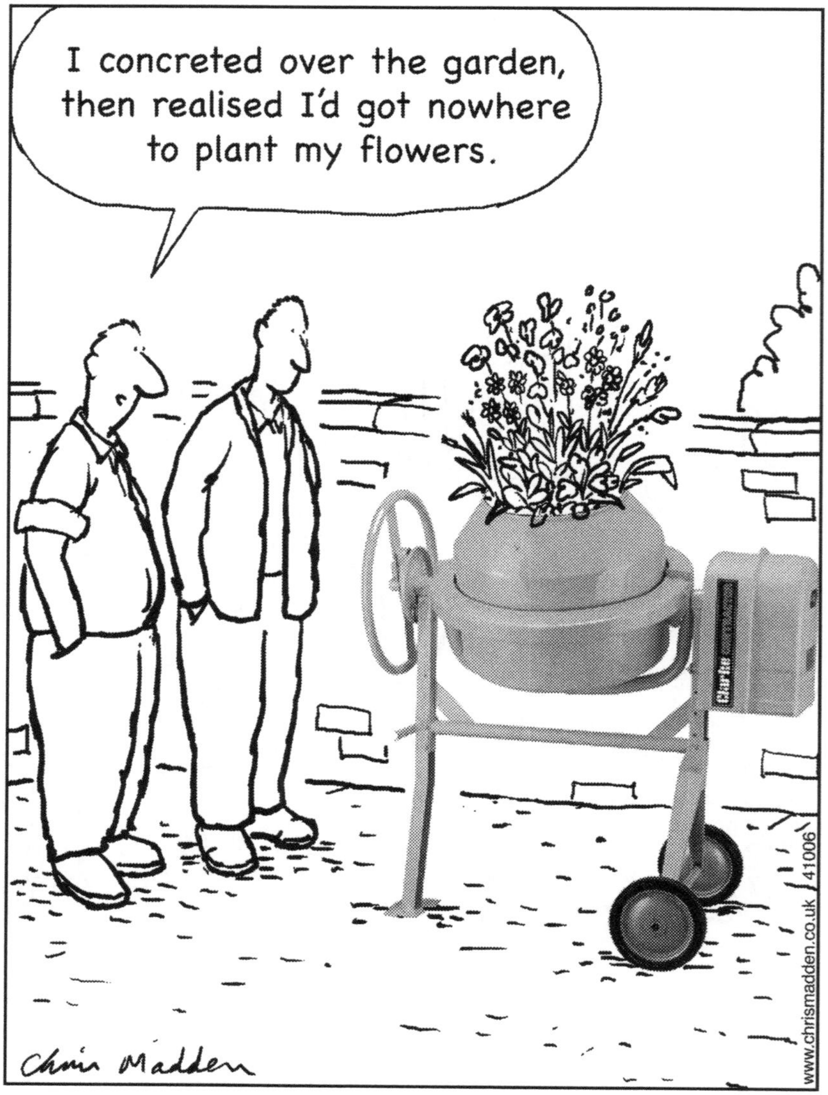
I concreted over the garden, then realised I'd got nowhere to plant my flowers.
Chris Madden
www.chrismadden.co.uk 41006

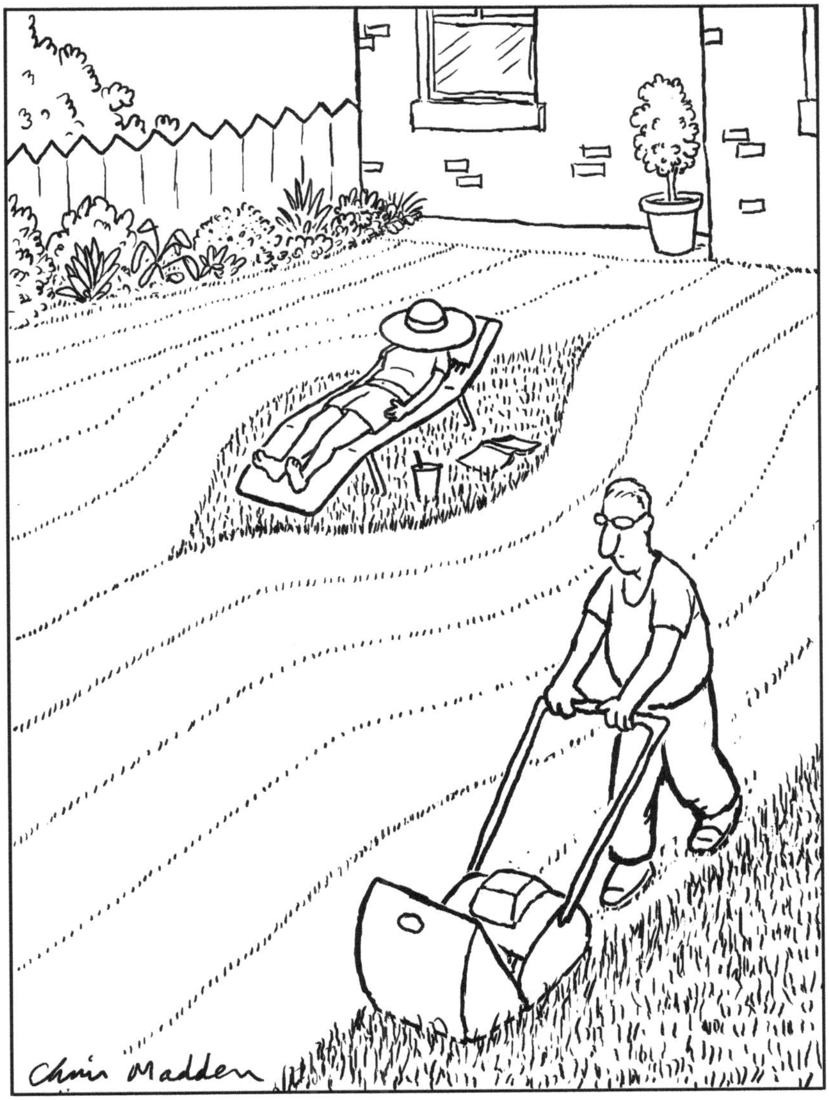
Chris Madden

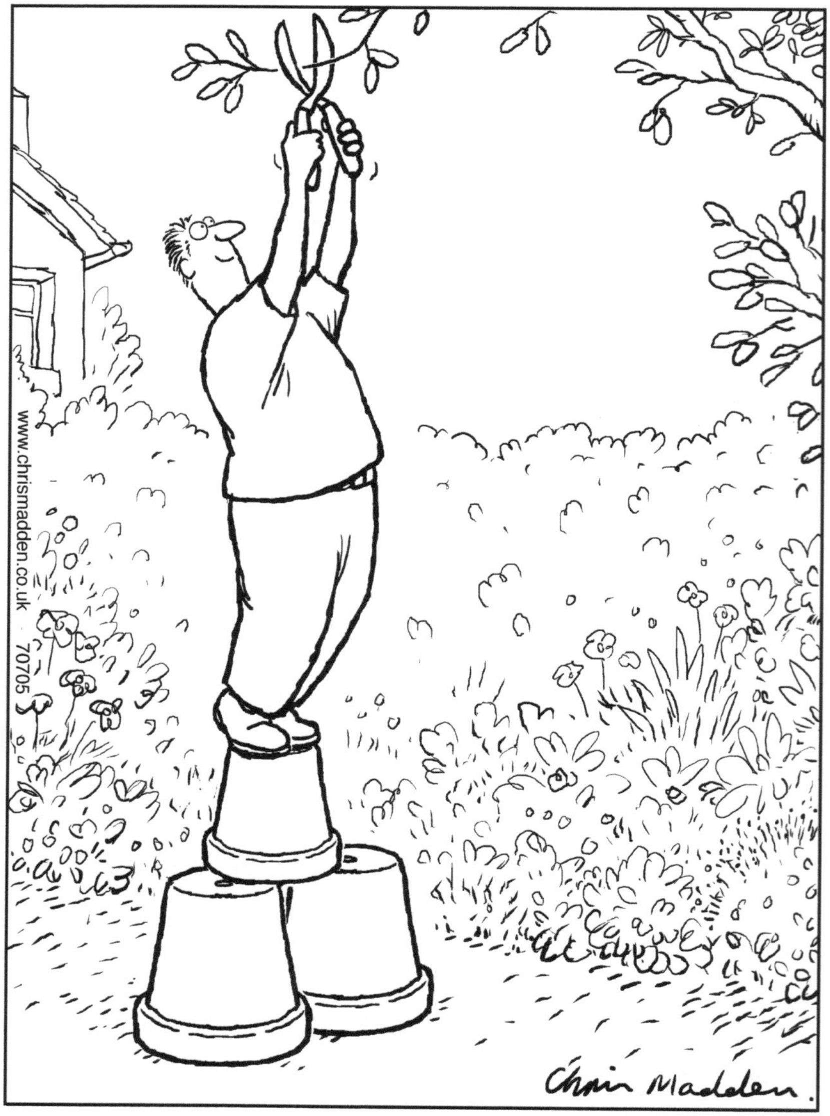
www.chrismadden.co.uk 70705
Chris Madden

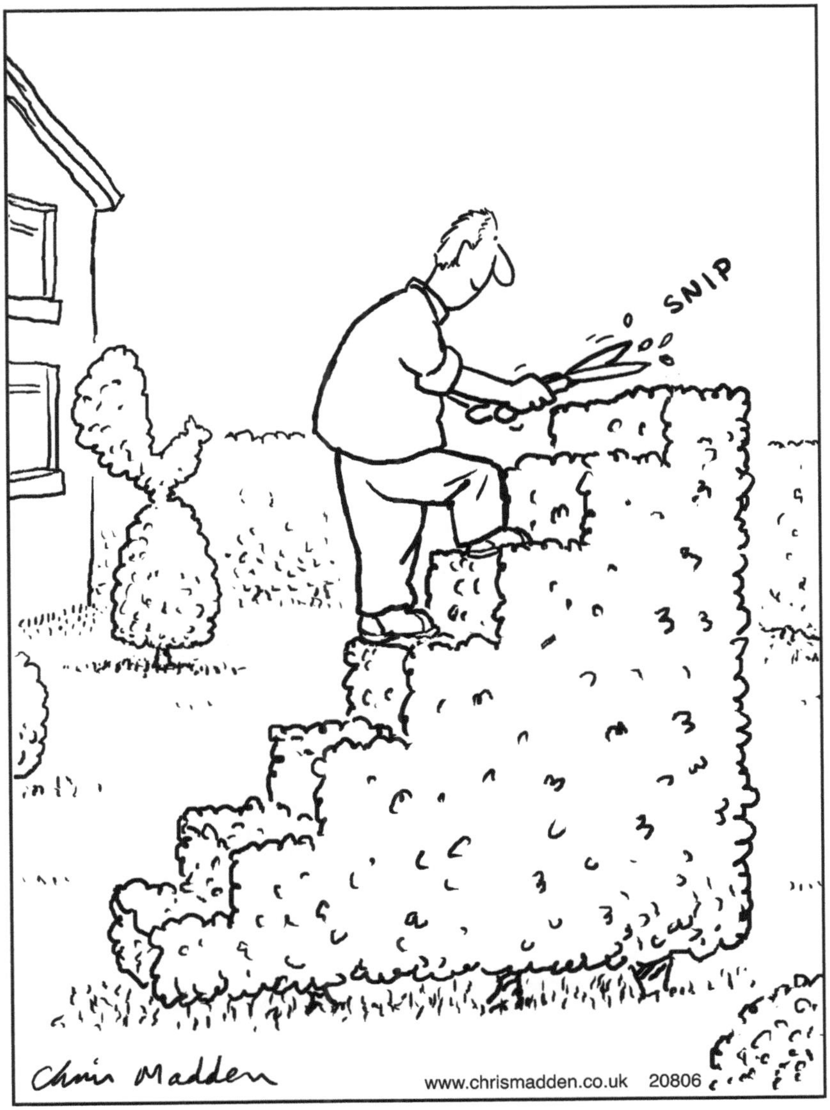
SNIP
Chris Madden
www.chrismadden.co.uk 20806

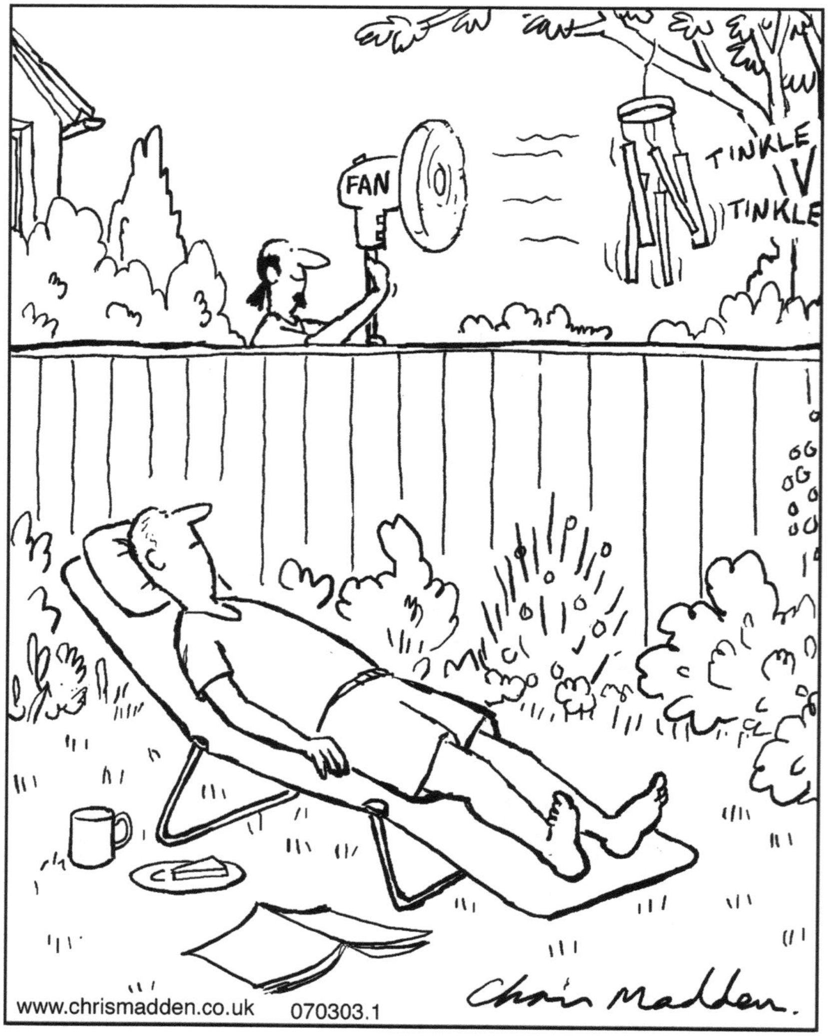
FAN
TINKLE
TINKLE
www.chrismadden.co.uk
070303.1
Chris Madden.

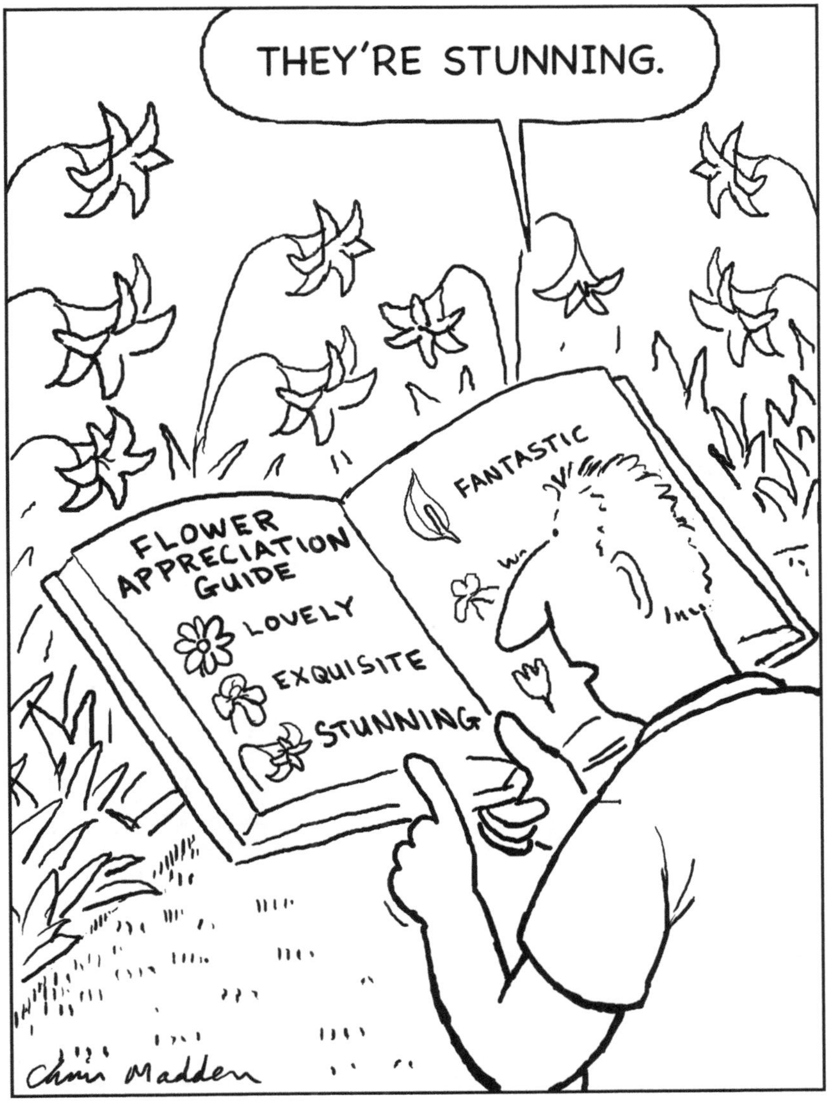
THEY'RE STUNNING.
FLOWER APPRECIATION GUIDE
LOVELY
EXQUISITE
STUNNING
FANTASTIC
Chris Madden

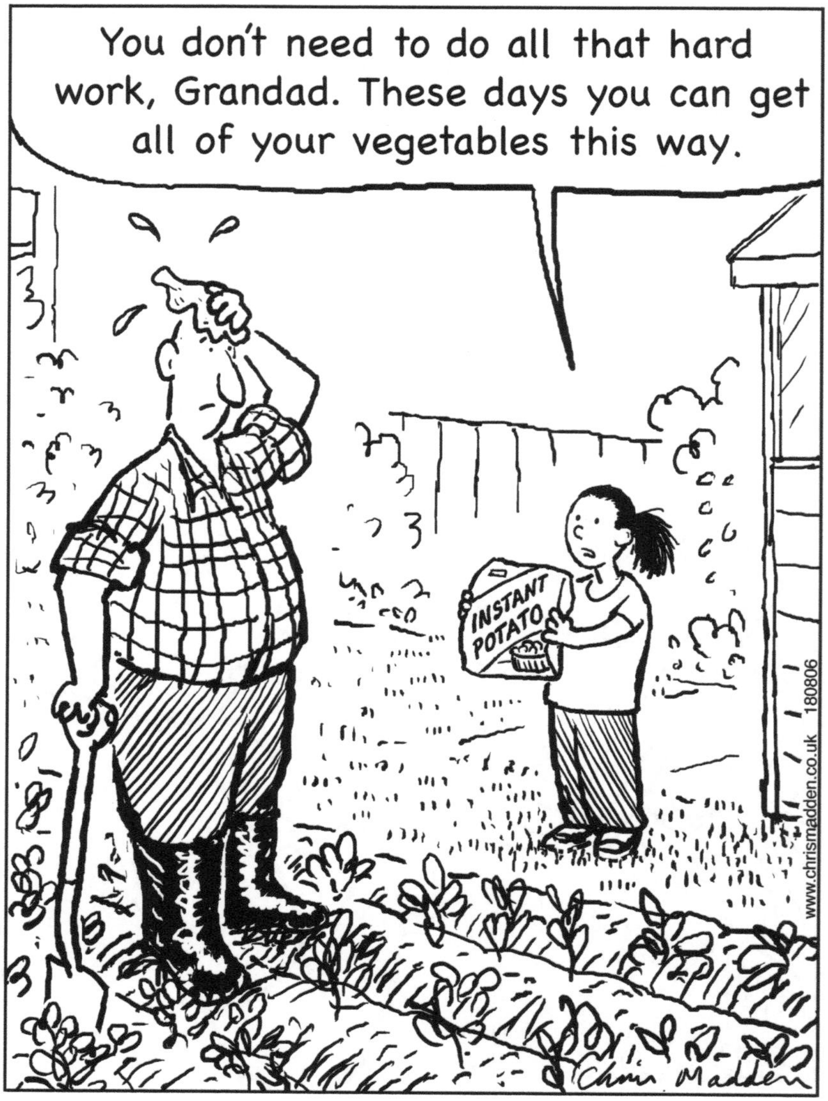
You don't need to do all that hard work, Grandad. These days you can get all of your vegetables this way.
INSTANT POTATO
www.chrismadden.co.uk 180806
Chris Madden

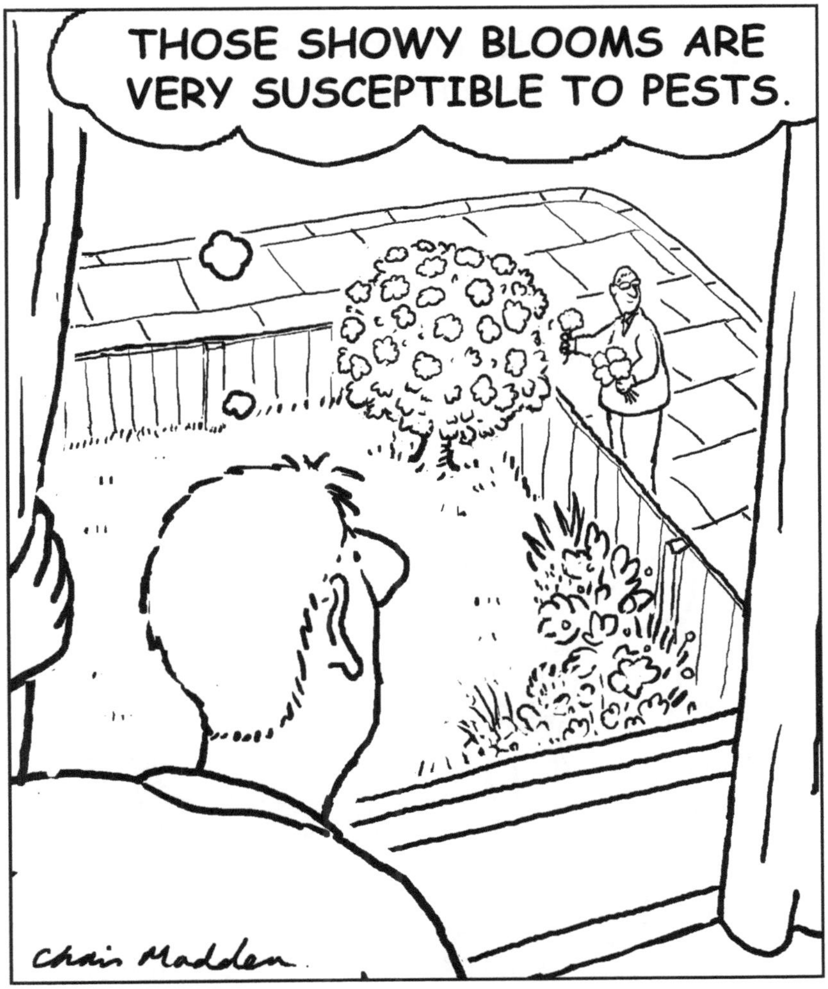
THOSE SHOWY BLOOMS ARE VERY SUSCEPTIBLE TO PESTS.
Chris Madden

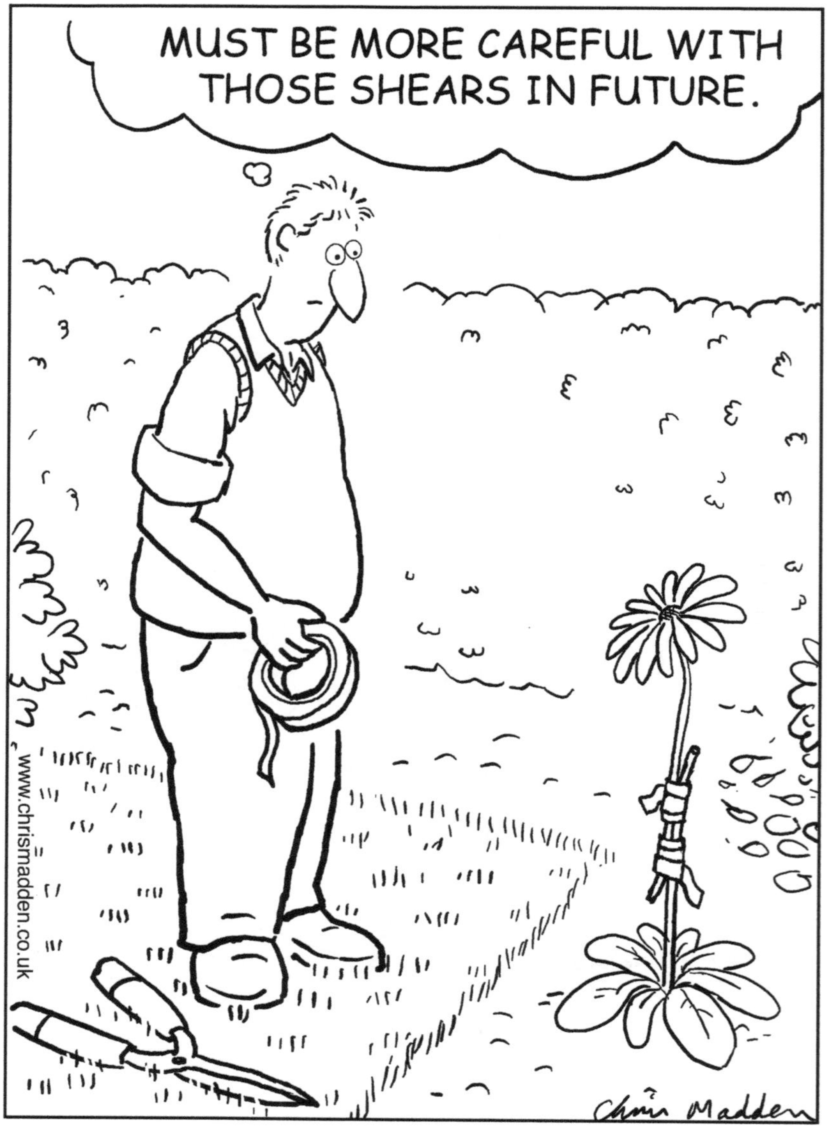
MUST BE MORE CAREFUL WITH THOSE SHEARS IN FUTURE.
www.chrismadden.co.uk
Chris Madden

HOW TO DEAL WITH WEEDS.

OBSERVE THE TRUE EXTENT
OF THE PROBLEM.

CHOOSE A PLEASANT DAY TO
DEVOTE TO YOUR ACTIVITY.

PUT ON OLD CLOTHES
AND STURDY FOOTWEAR.

GO FOR A NICE WALK
IN THE COUNTRYSIDE.

Chris Madden

73

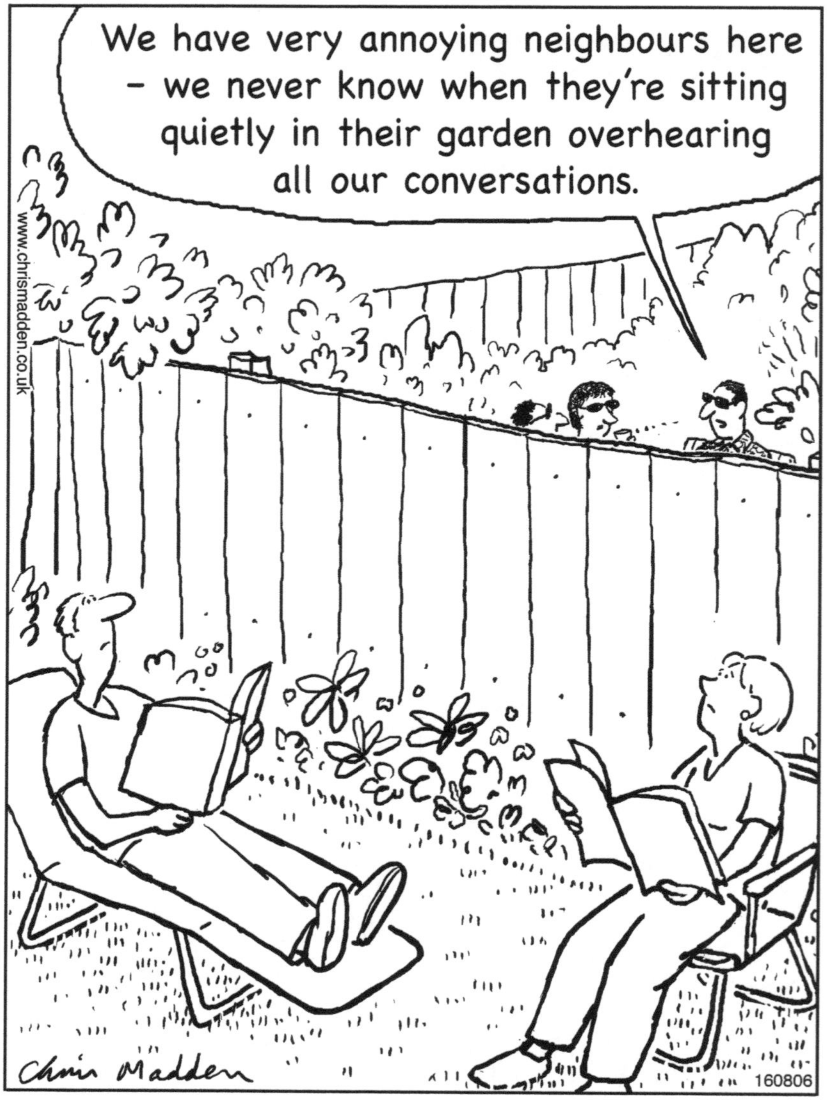
We have very annoying neighbours here – we never know when they're sitting quietly in their garden overhearing all our conversations.
www.chrismadden.co.uk
Chris Madden
160806

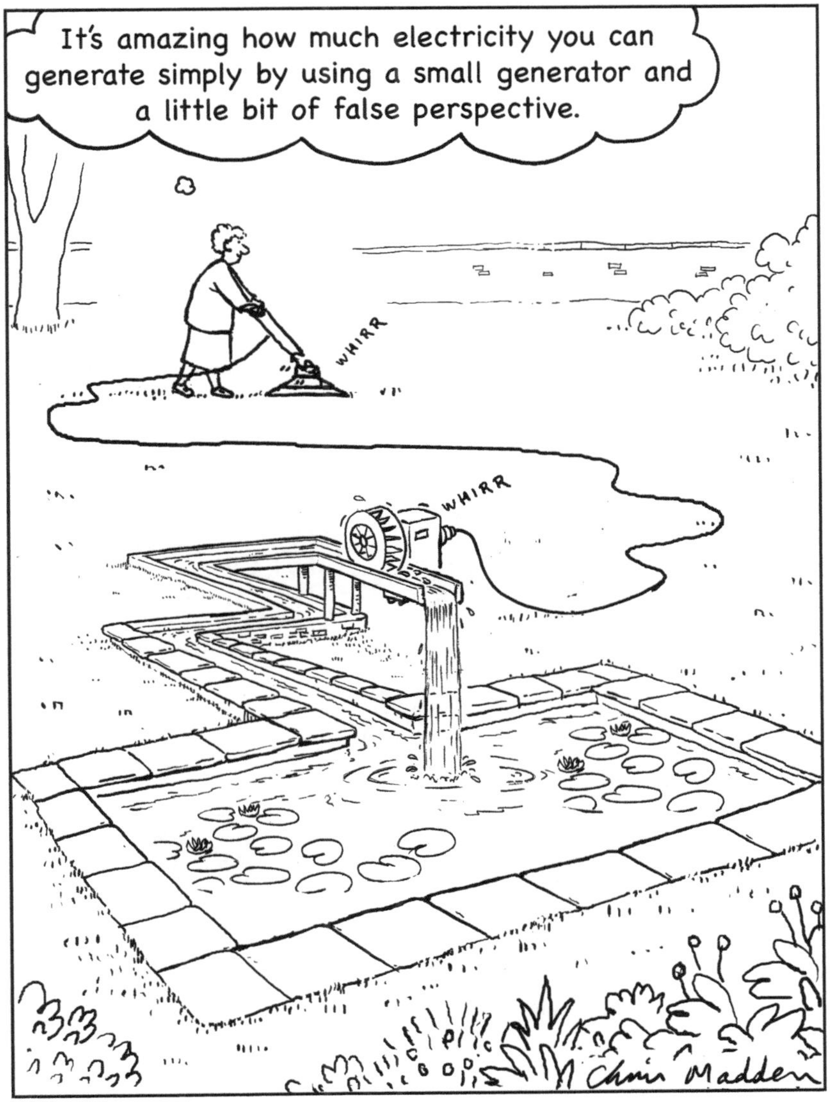
It's amazing how much electricity you can generate simply by using a small generator and a little bit of false perspective.
WHIRR
WHIRR
Chris Madden

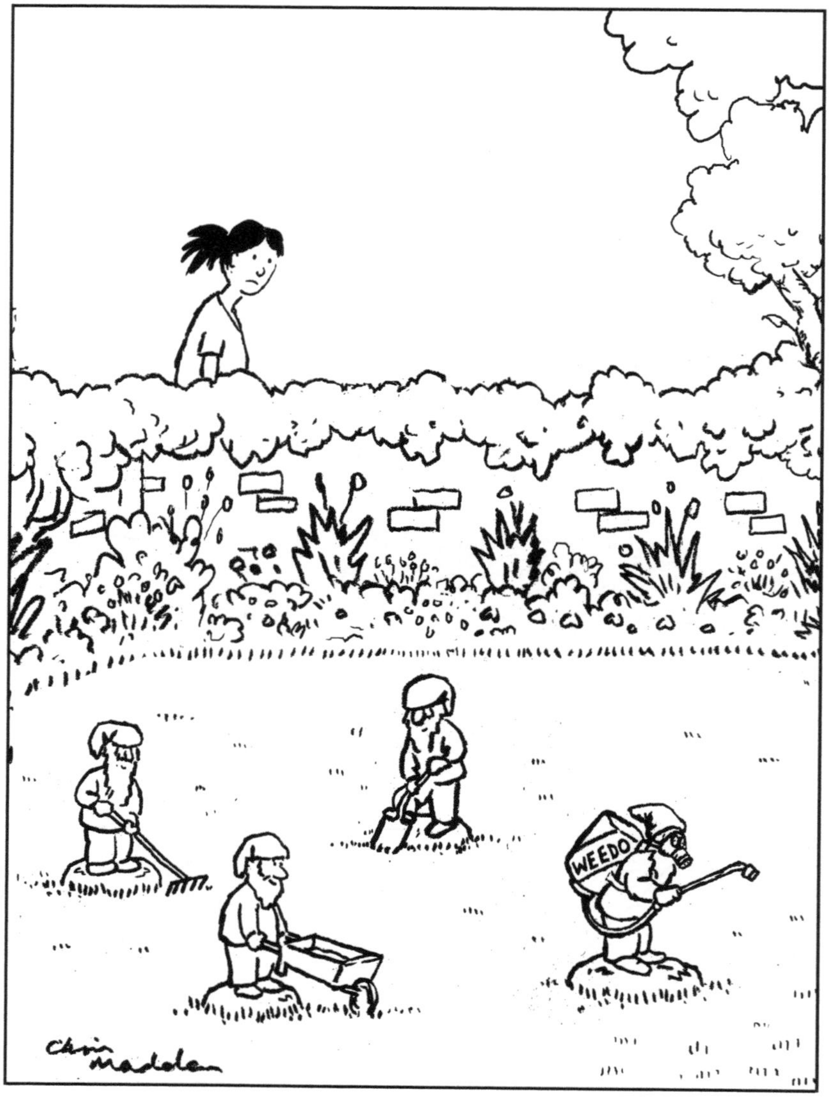
WEEDO
Chris Madden

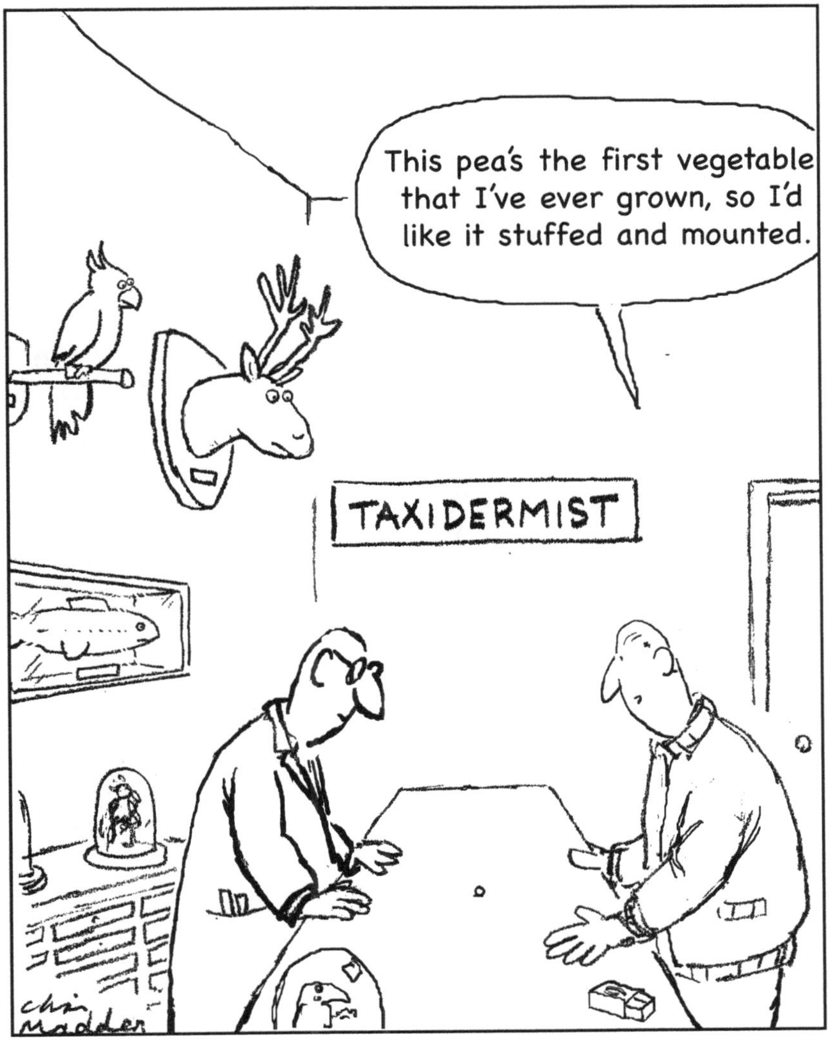
This pea's the first vegetable that I've ever grown, so I'd like it stuffed and mounted.
TAXIDERMIST

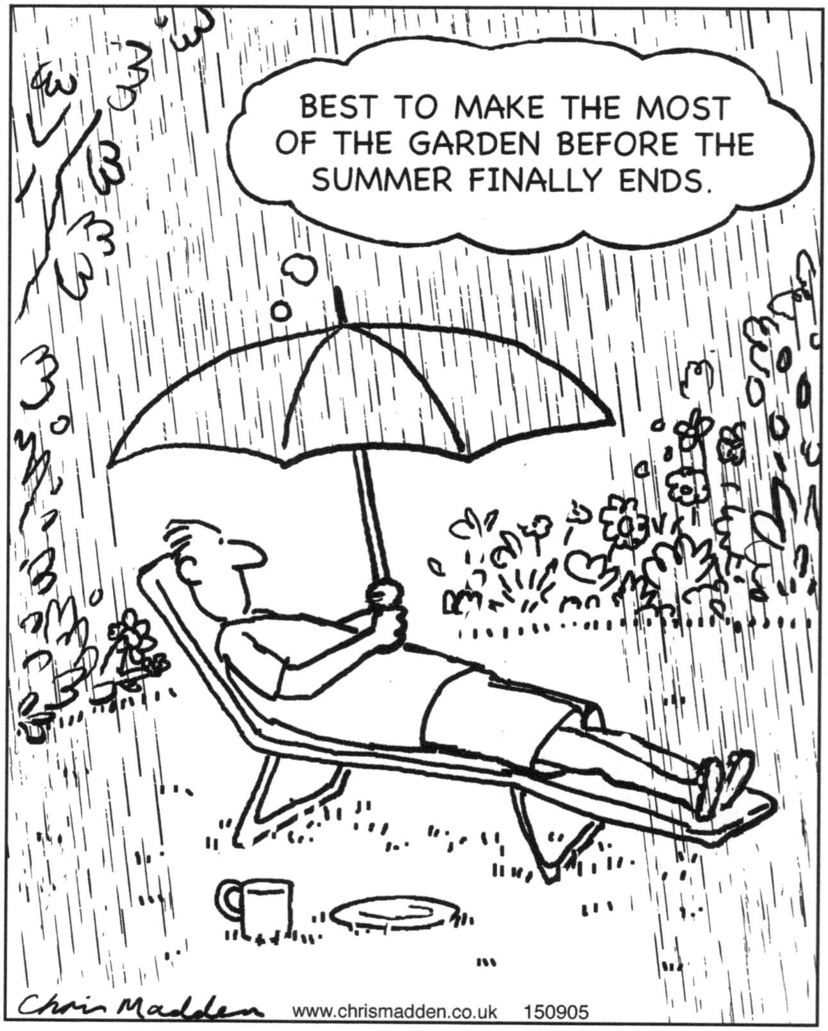
BEST TO MAKE THE MOST OF THE GARDEN BEFORE THE SUMMER FINALLY ENDS.
Chris Madden
www.chrismadden.co.uk 150905

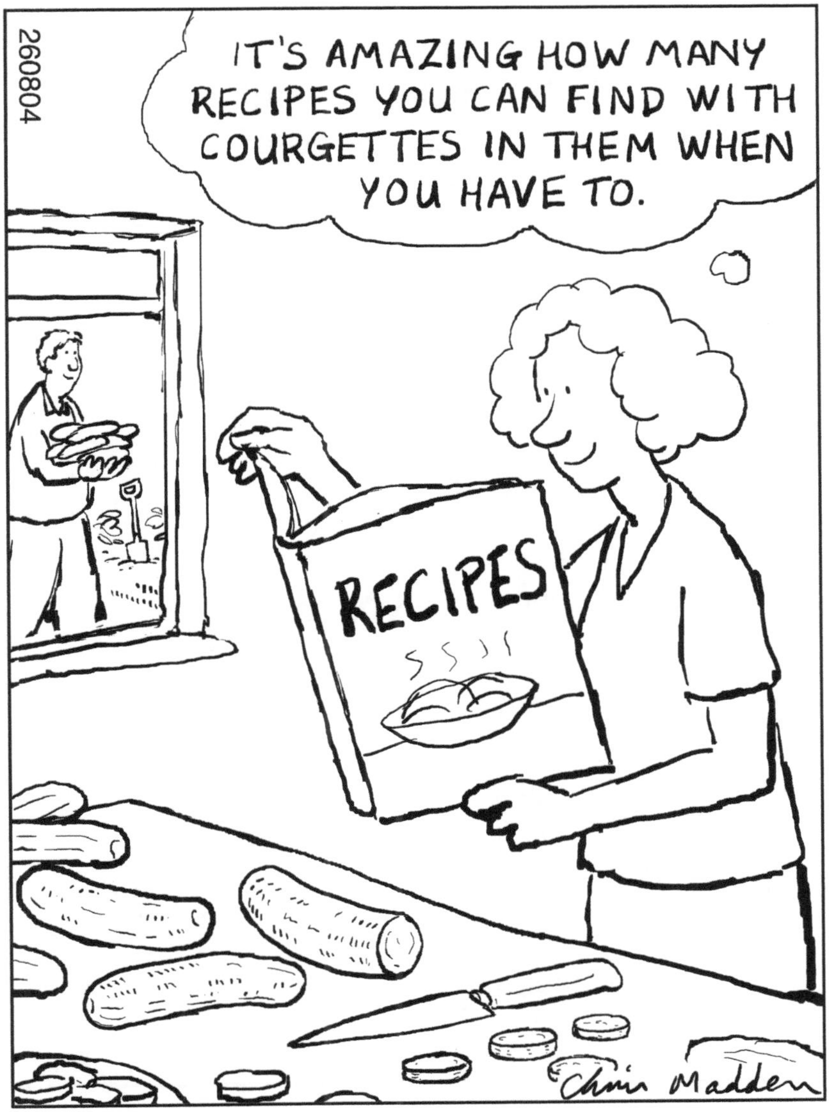
260804
IT'S AMAZING HOW MANY RECIPES YOU CAN FIND WITH COURGETTES IN THEM WHEN YOU HAVE TO.
RECIPES
Chris Madden

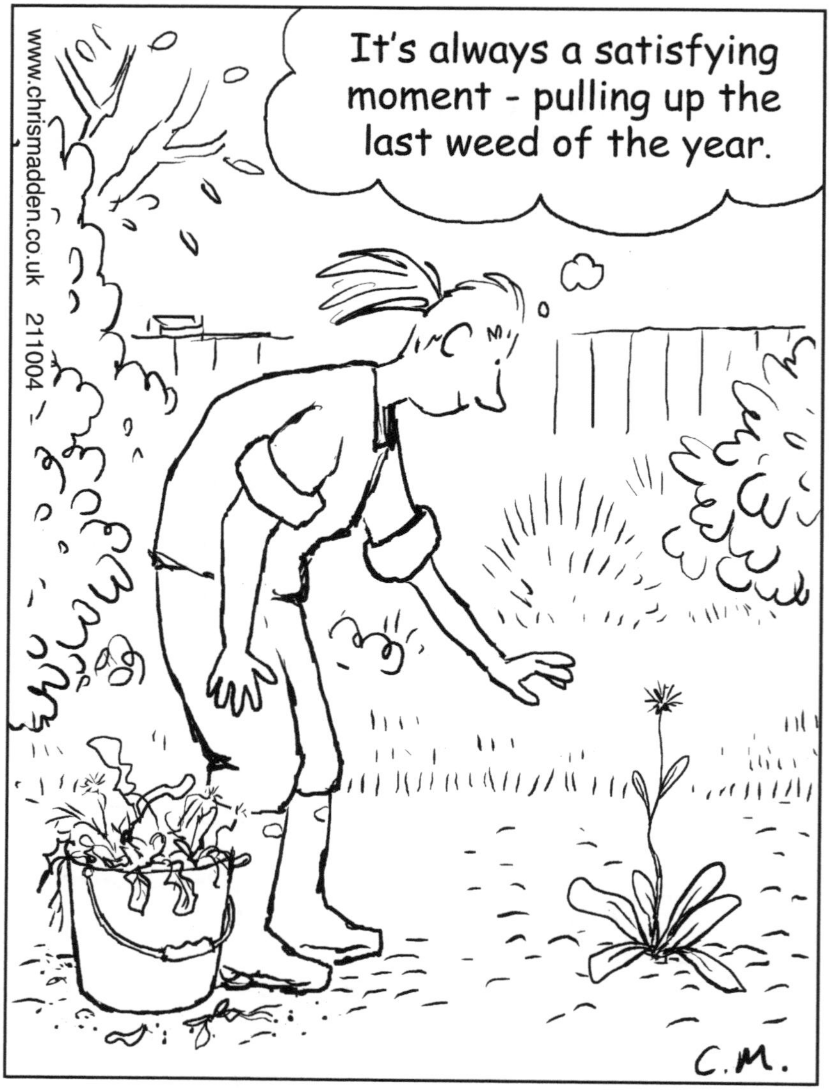
It's always a satisfying moment - pulling up the last weed of the year.
www.chrismadden.co.uk 211004
C.M.

AUTUMN

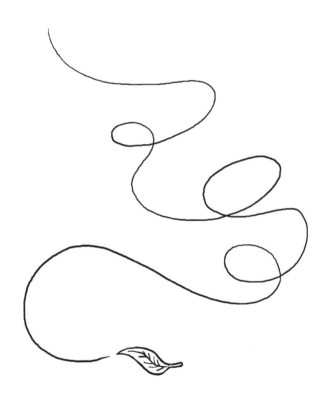

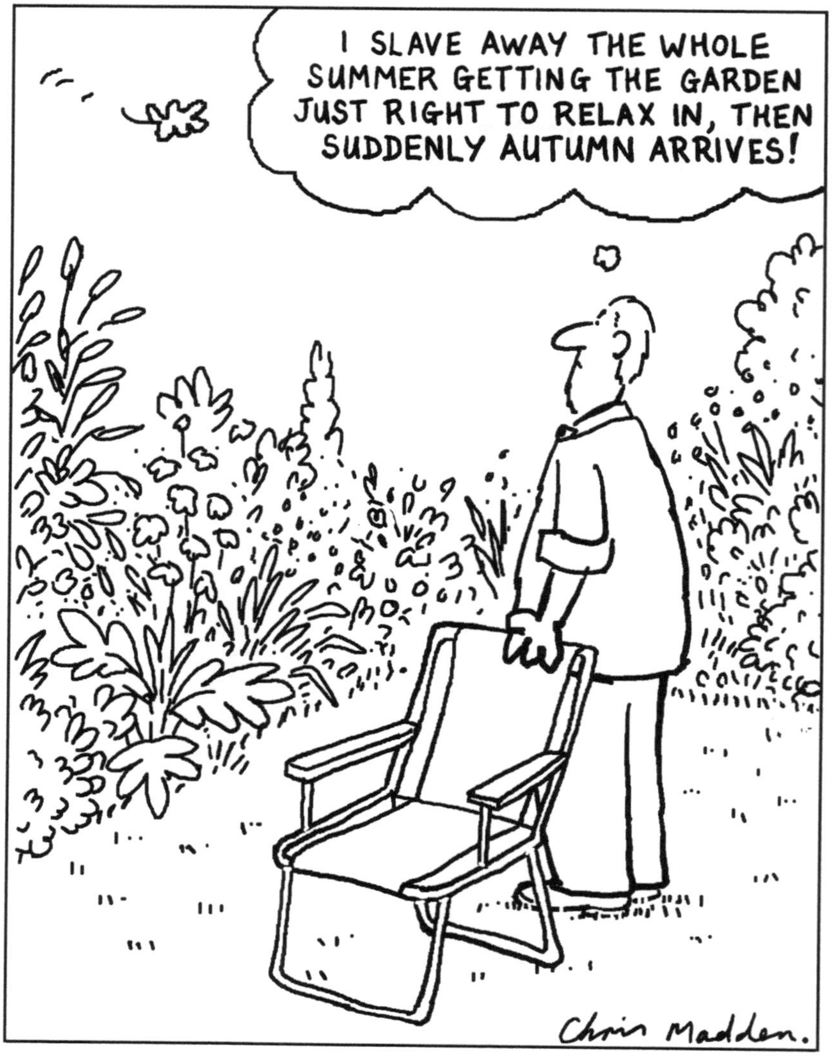
I SLAVE AWAY THE WHOLE SUMMER GETTING THE GARDEN JUST RIGHT TO RELAX IN, THEN SUDDENLY AUTUMN ARRIVES!
Chris Madden.

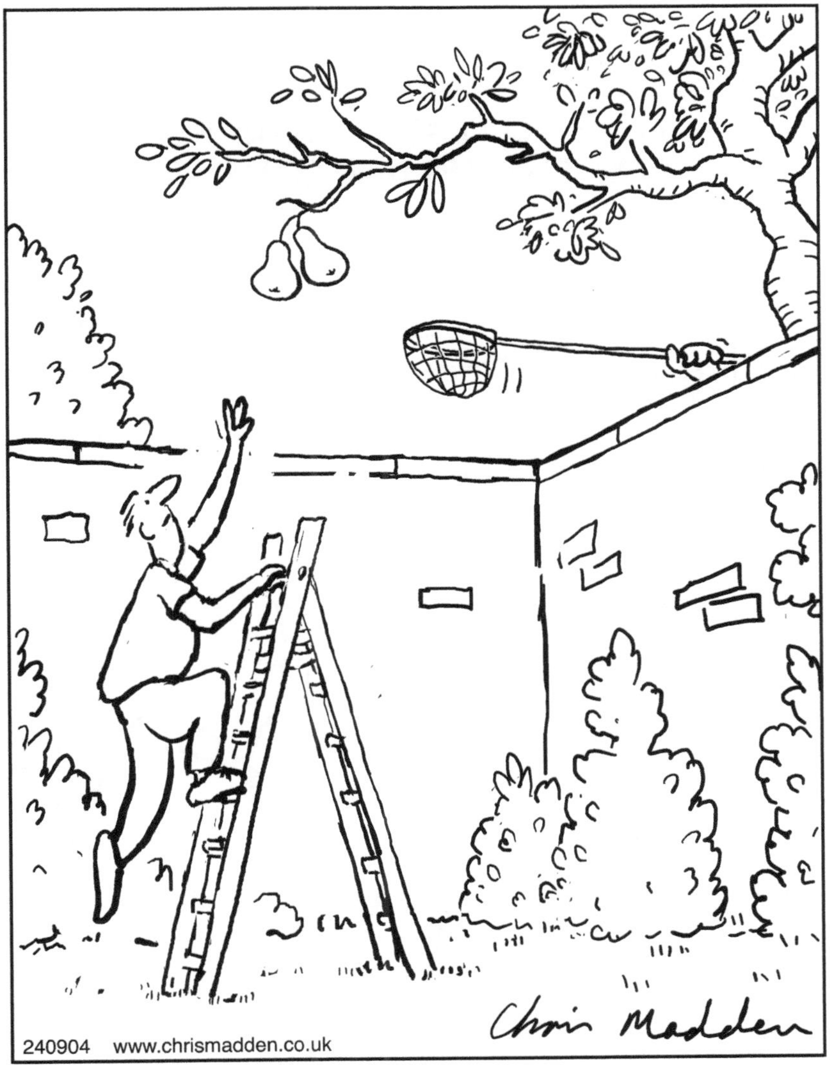
Chris Madden
240904 www.chrismadden.co.uk

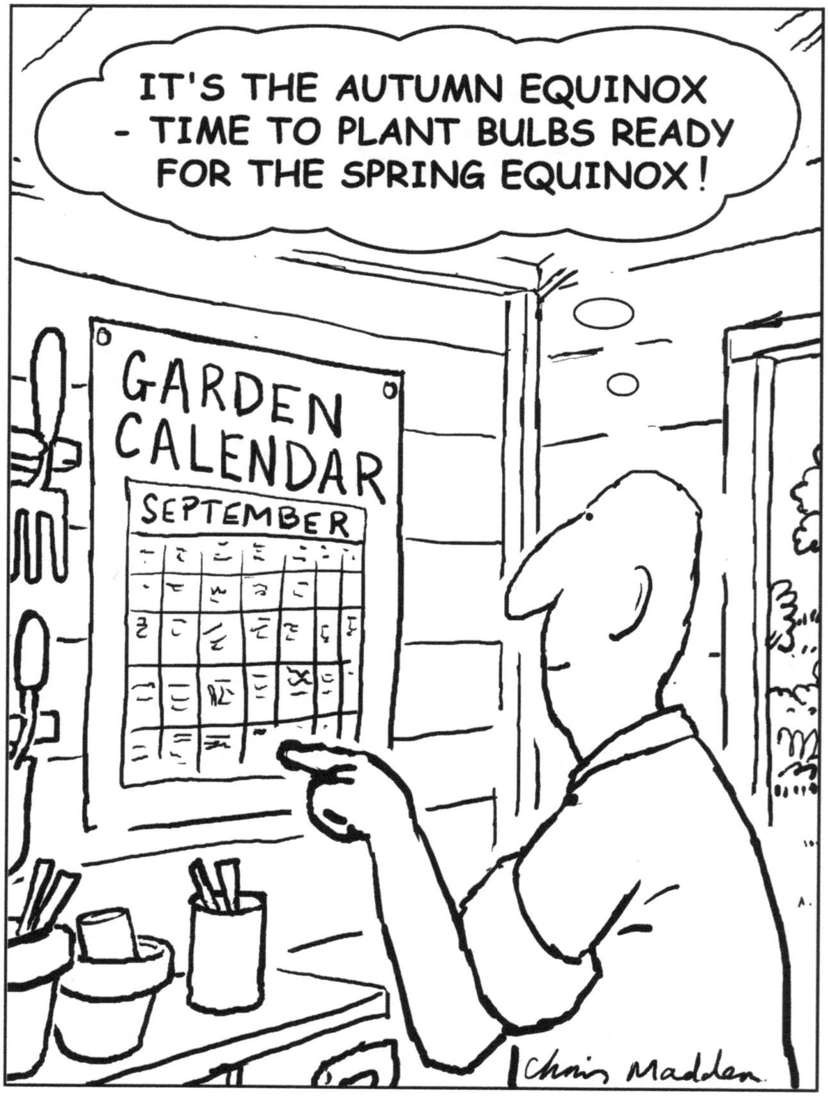
IT'S THE AUTUMN EQUINOX - TIME TO PLANT BULBS READY FOR THE SPRING EQUINOX!
GARDEN CALENDAR
SEPTEMBER
Chris Madden

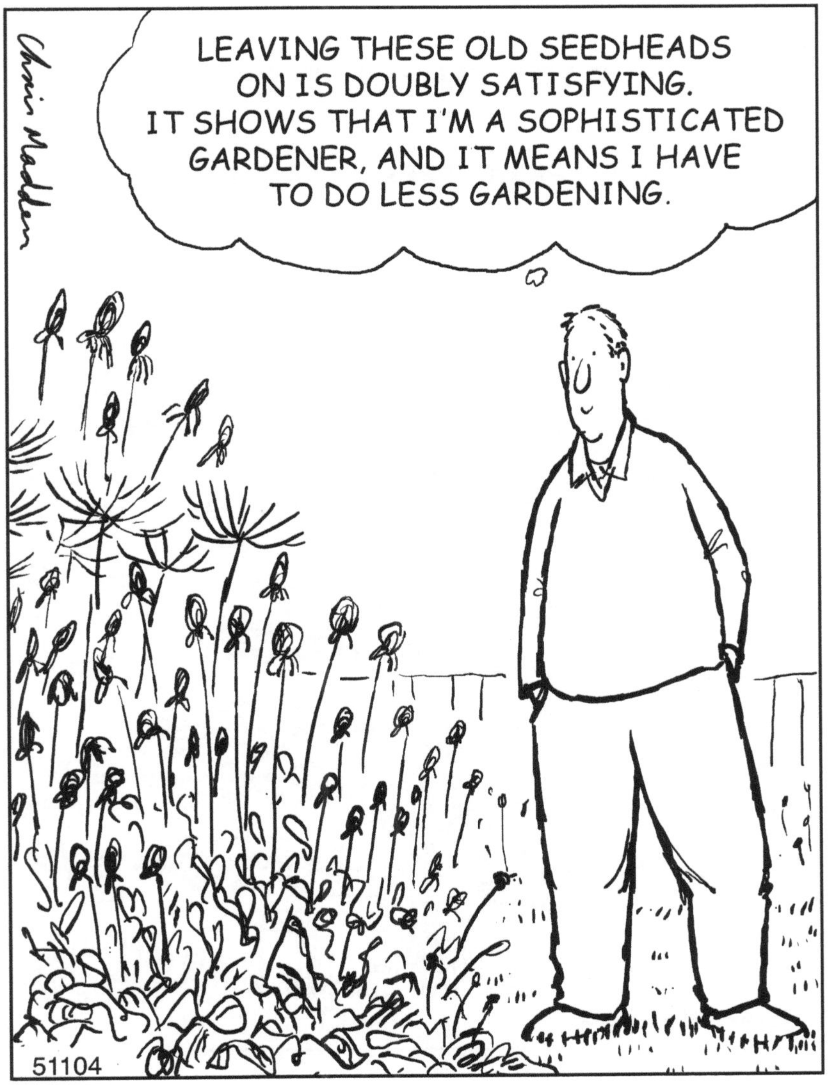
LEAVING THESE OLD SEEDHEADS ON IS DOUBLY SATISFYING. IT SHOWS THAT I'M A SOPHISTICATED GARDENER, AND IT MEANS I HAVE TO DO LESS GARDENING.
Chris Madden
51104

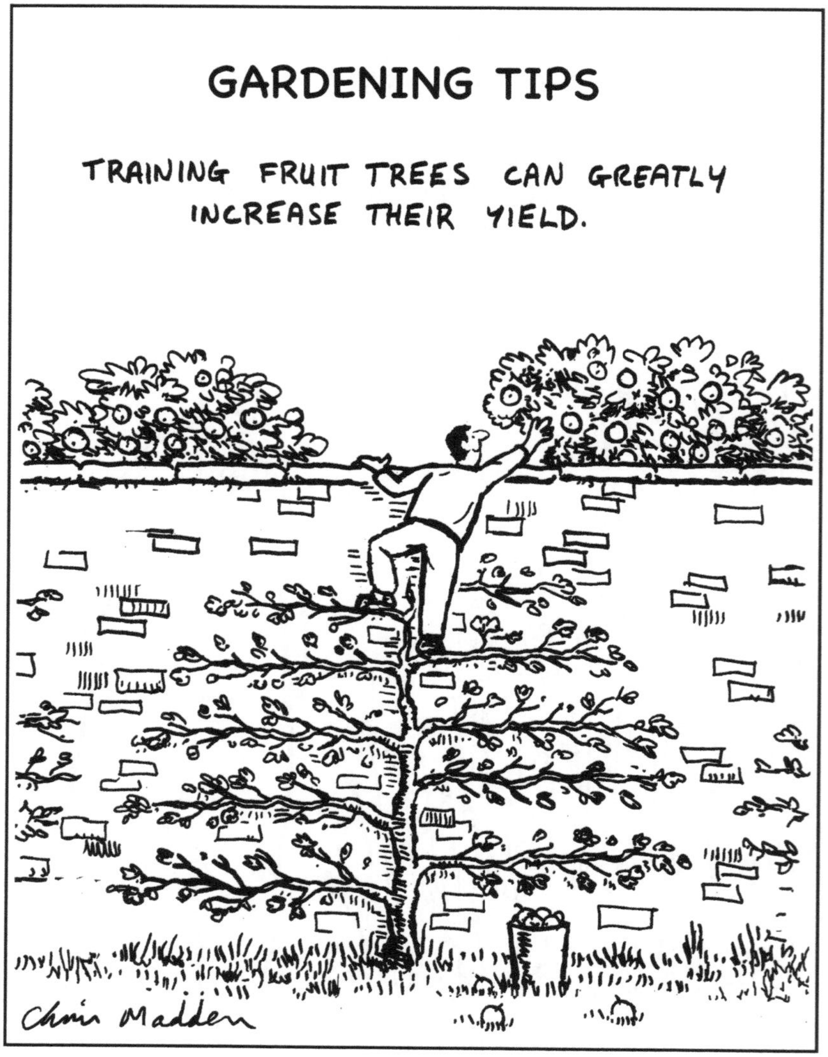
GARDENING TIPS
TRAINING FRUIT TREES CAN GREATLY INCREASE THEIR YIELD.
Chris Madden

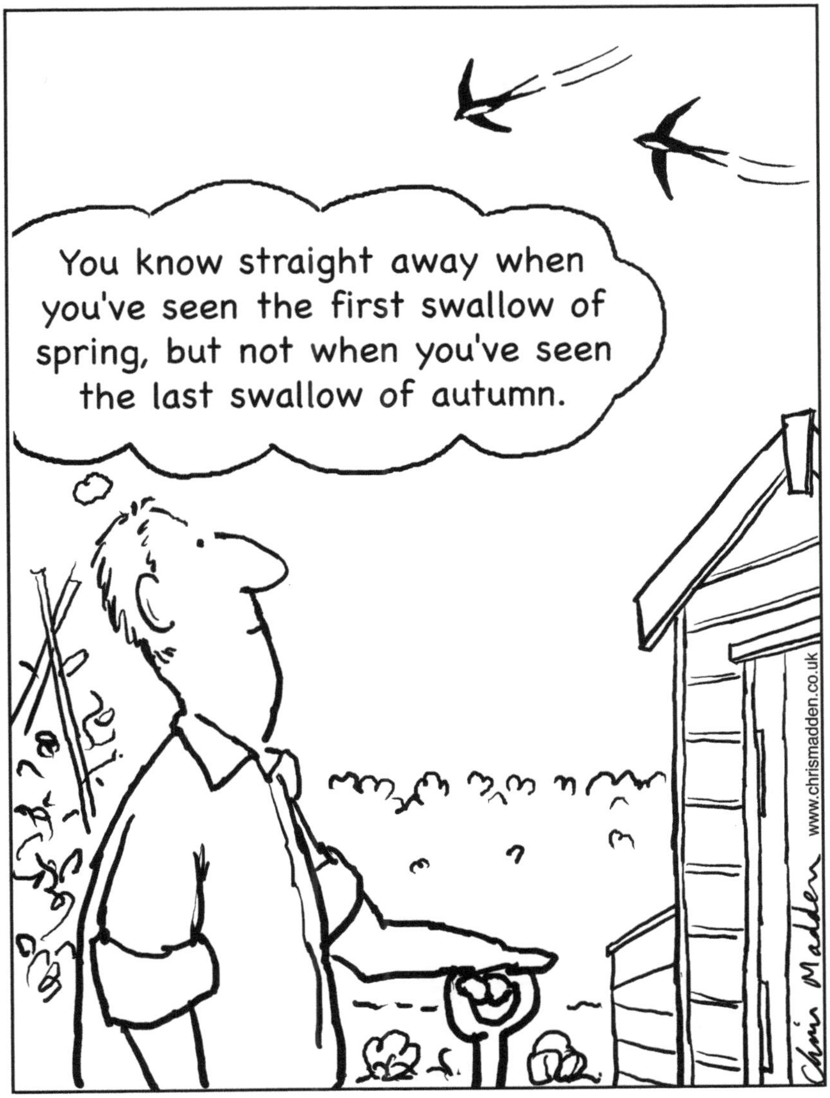
You know straight away when you've seen the first swallow of spring, but not when you've seen the last swallow of autumn.
Chris Madden
www.chrismadden.co.uk

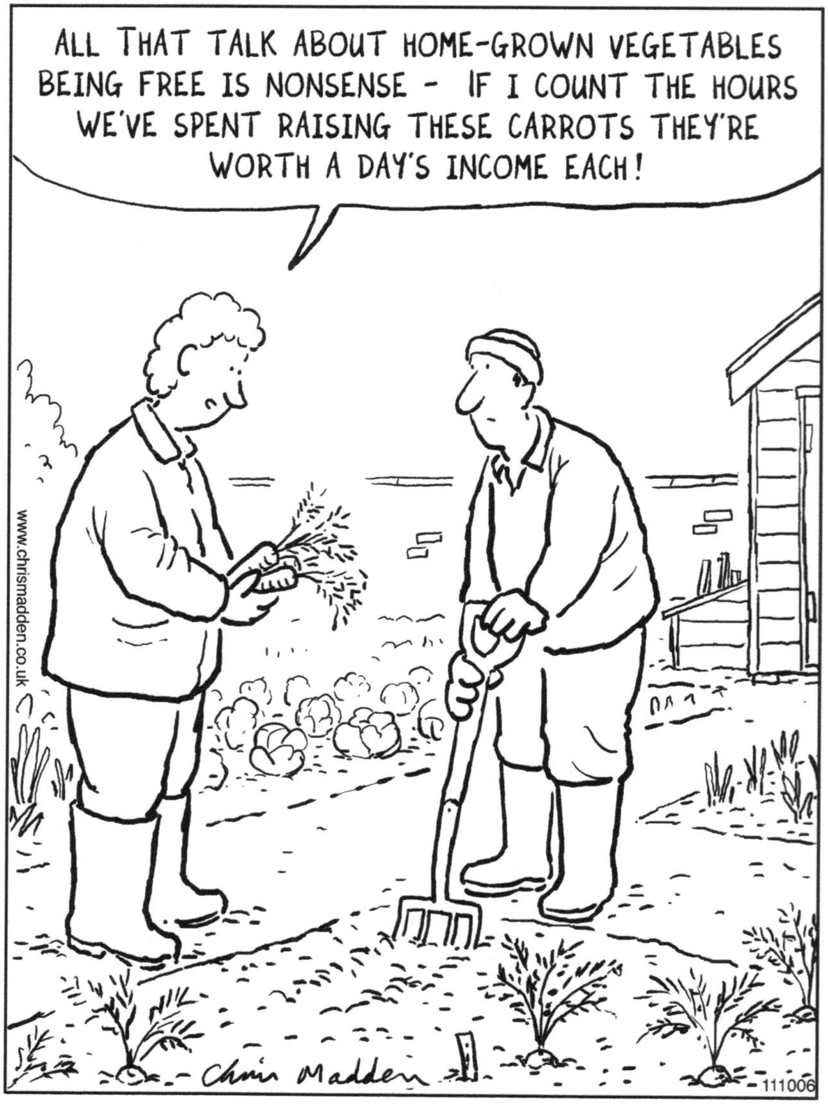
ALL THAT TALK ABOUT HOME-GROWN VEGETABLES BEING FREE IS NONSENSE - IF I COUNT THE HOURS WE'VE SPENT RAISING THESE CARROTS THEY'RE WORTH A DAY'S INCOME EACH!
www.chrismadden.co.uk
Chris Madden
111006

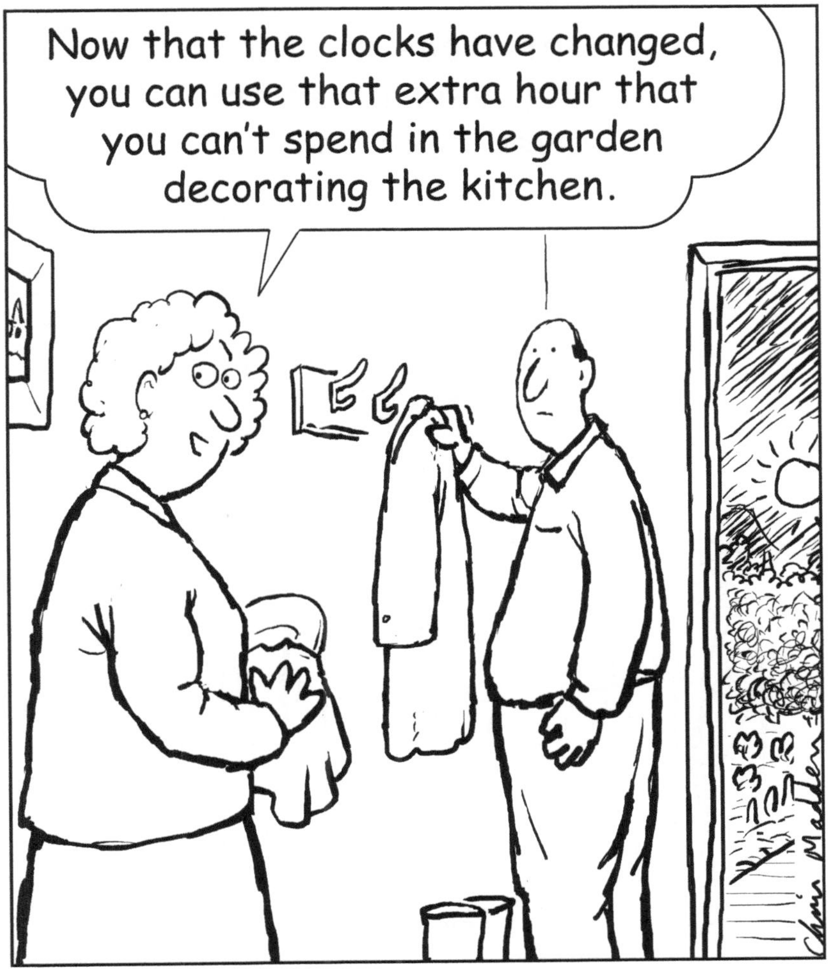
Now that the clocks have changed, you can use that extra hour that you can't spend in the garden decorating the kitchen.

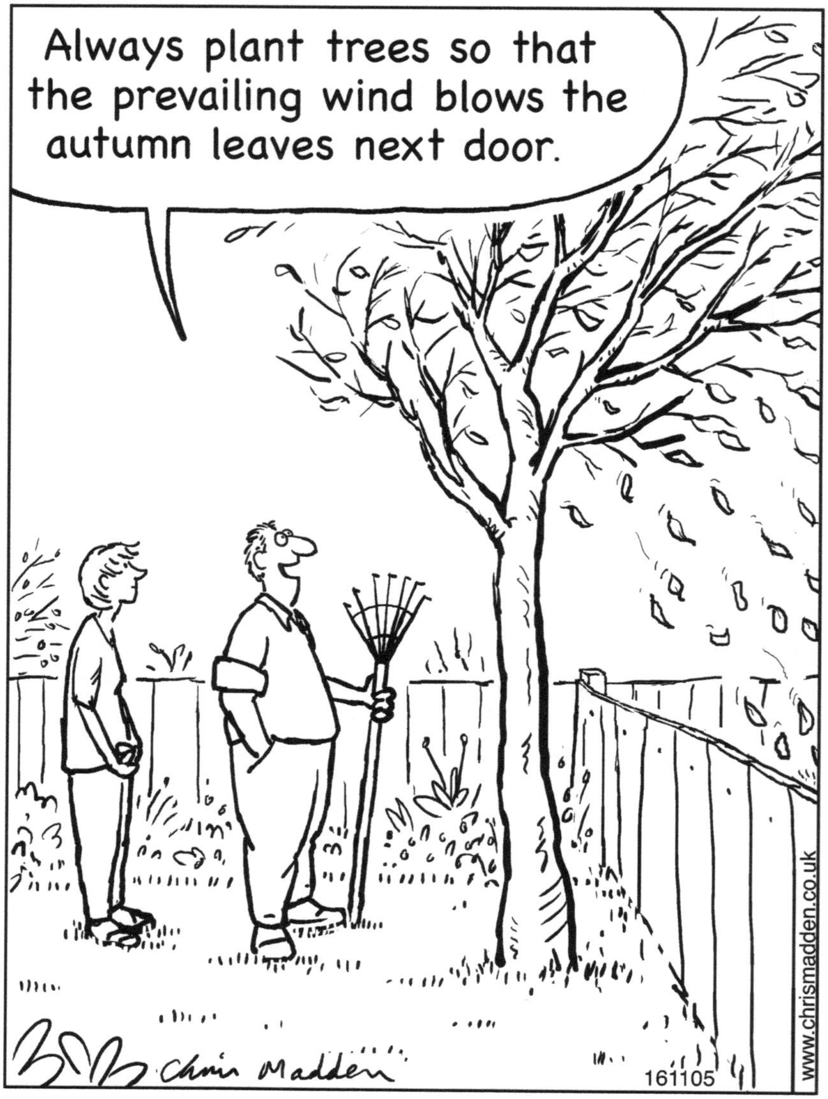
Always plant trees so that the prevailing wind blows the autumn leaves next door.
Chris Madden
161105
www.chrismadden.co.uk

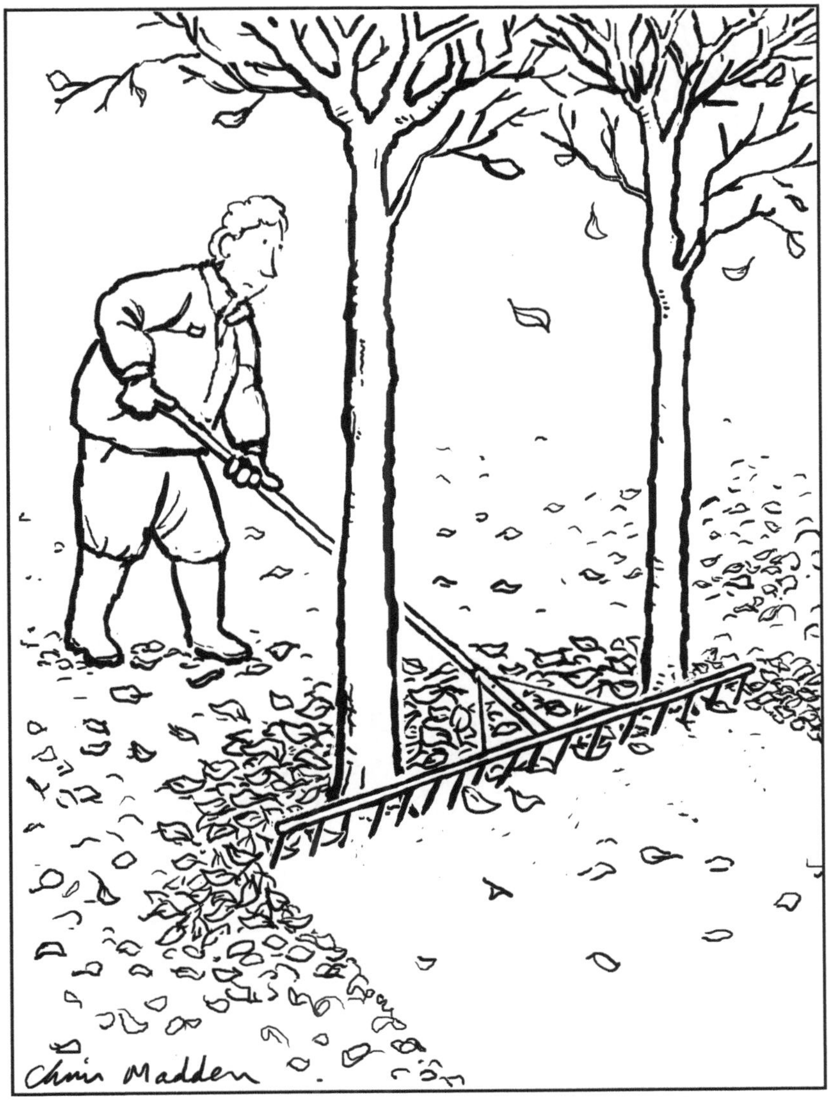
Chris Madden

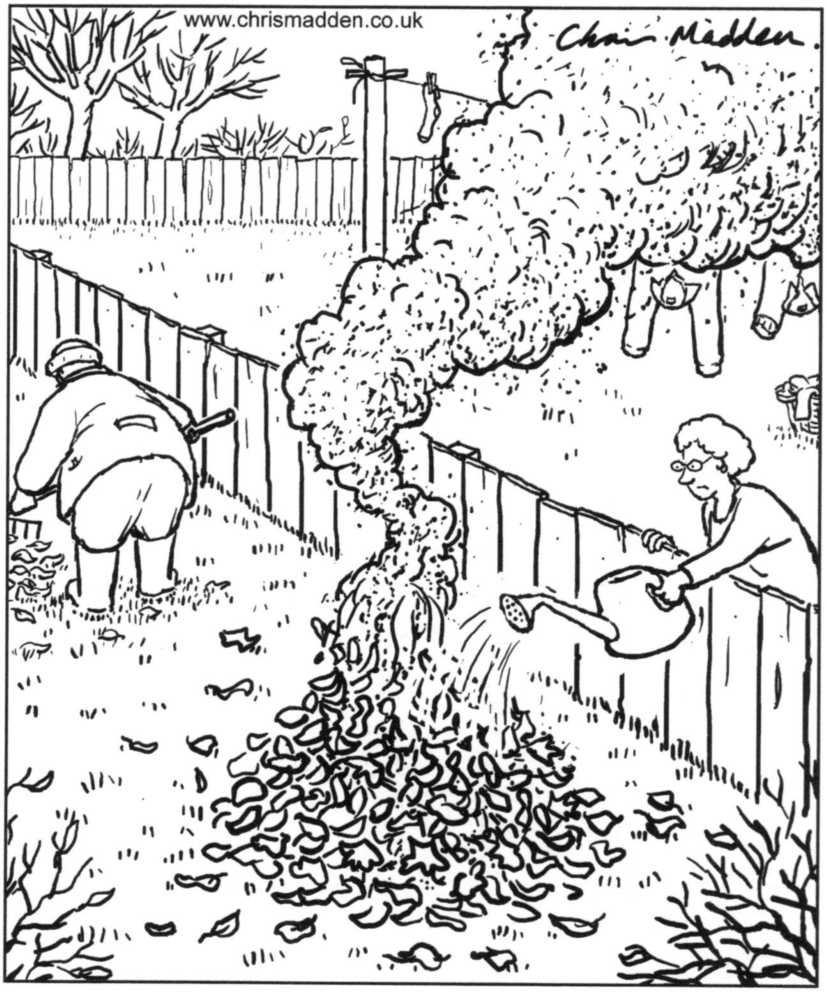
www.chrismadden.co.uk
Chris Madden

WINTER

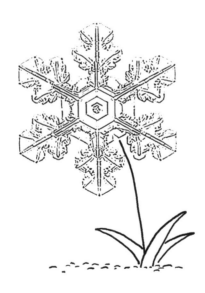

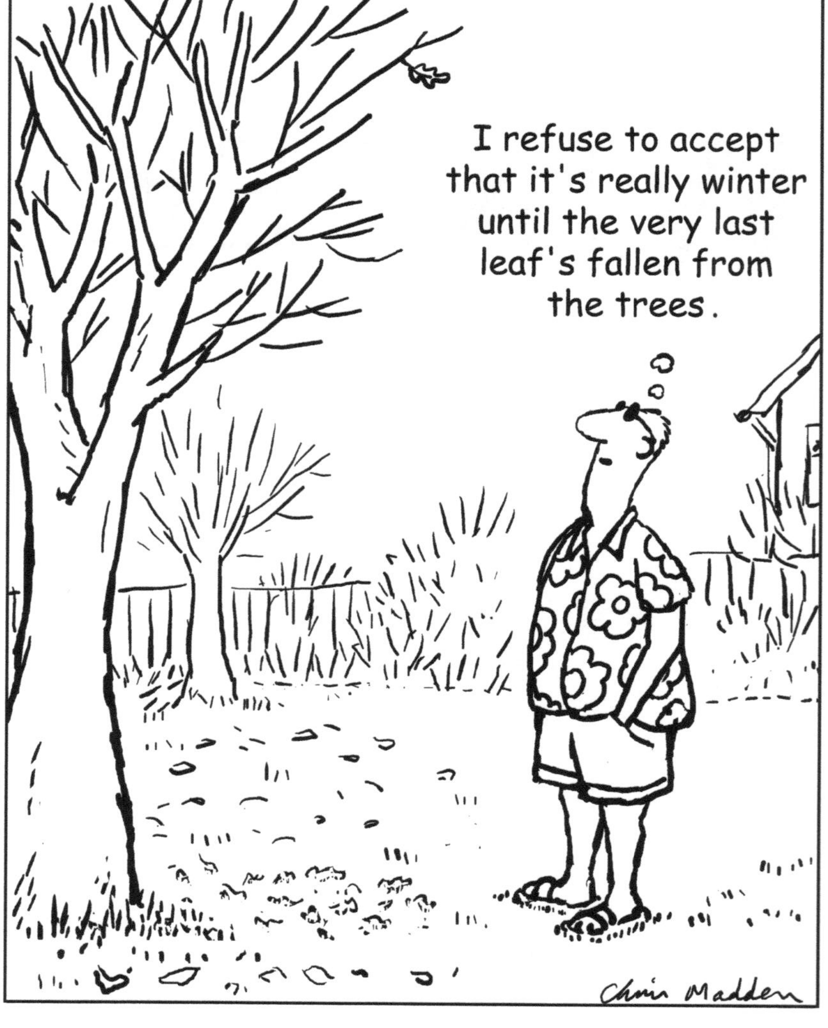
I refuse to accept that it's really winter until the very last leaf's fallen from the trees.
Chris Madden

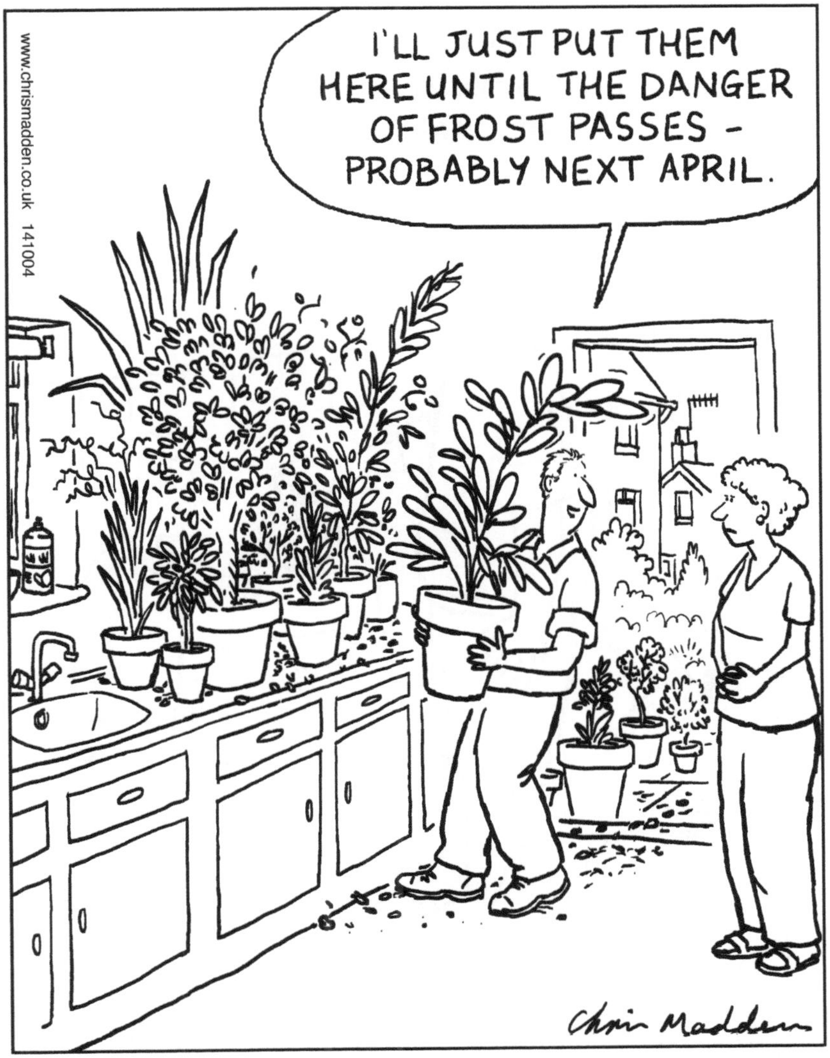
I'LL JUST PUT THEM HERE UNTIL THE DANGER OF FROST PASSES - PROBABLY NEXT APRIL.
www.chrismadden.co.uk 141004
Chris Madden

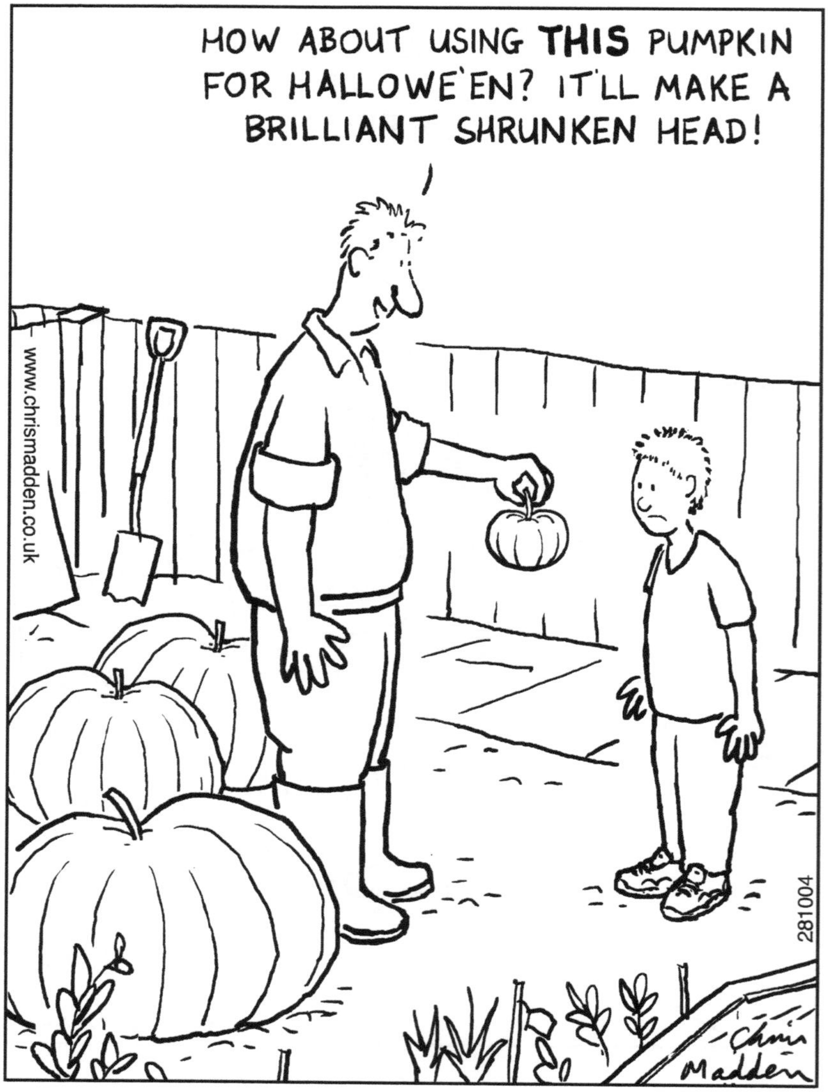
HOW ABOUT USING **THIS** PUMPKIN FOR HALLOWE'EN? IT'LL MAKE A BRILLIANT SHRUNKEN HEAD!
www.chrismadden.co.uk
281004
Chris Madden

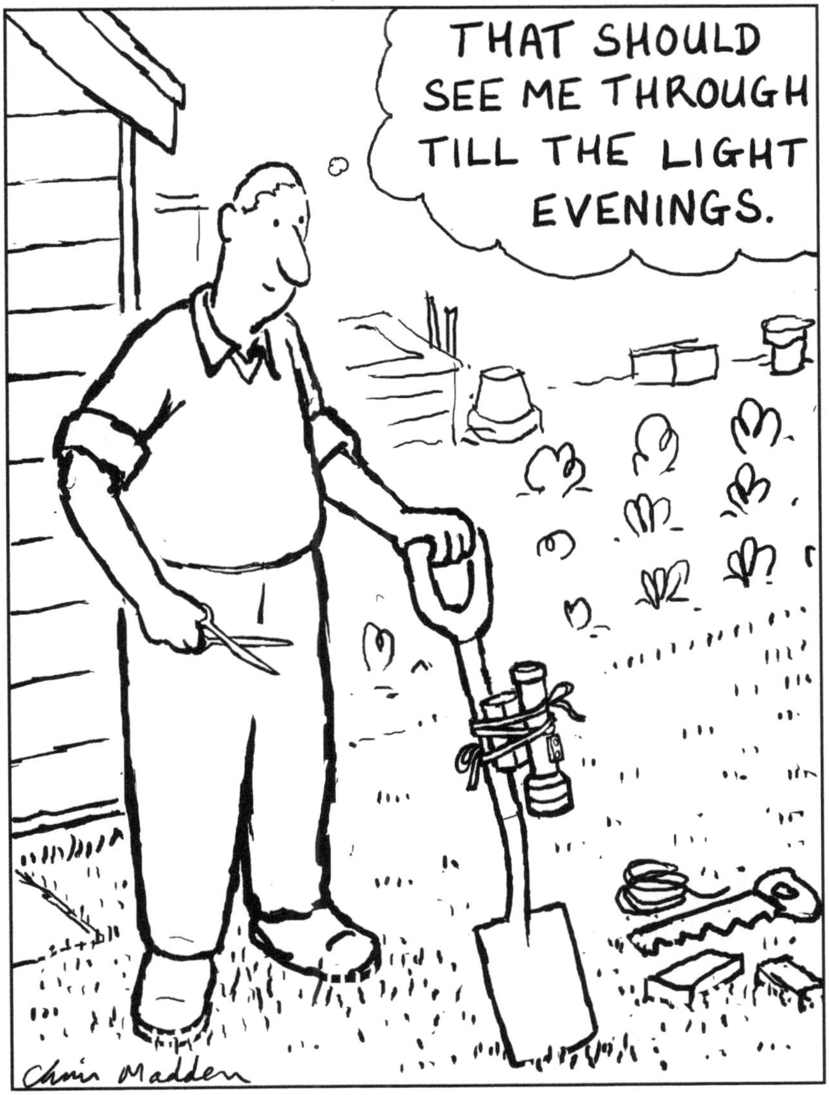
THAT SHOULD SEE ME THROUGH TILL THE LIGHT EVENINGS.
Chris Madden

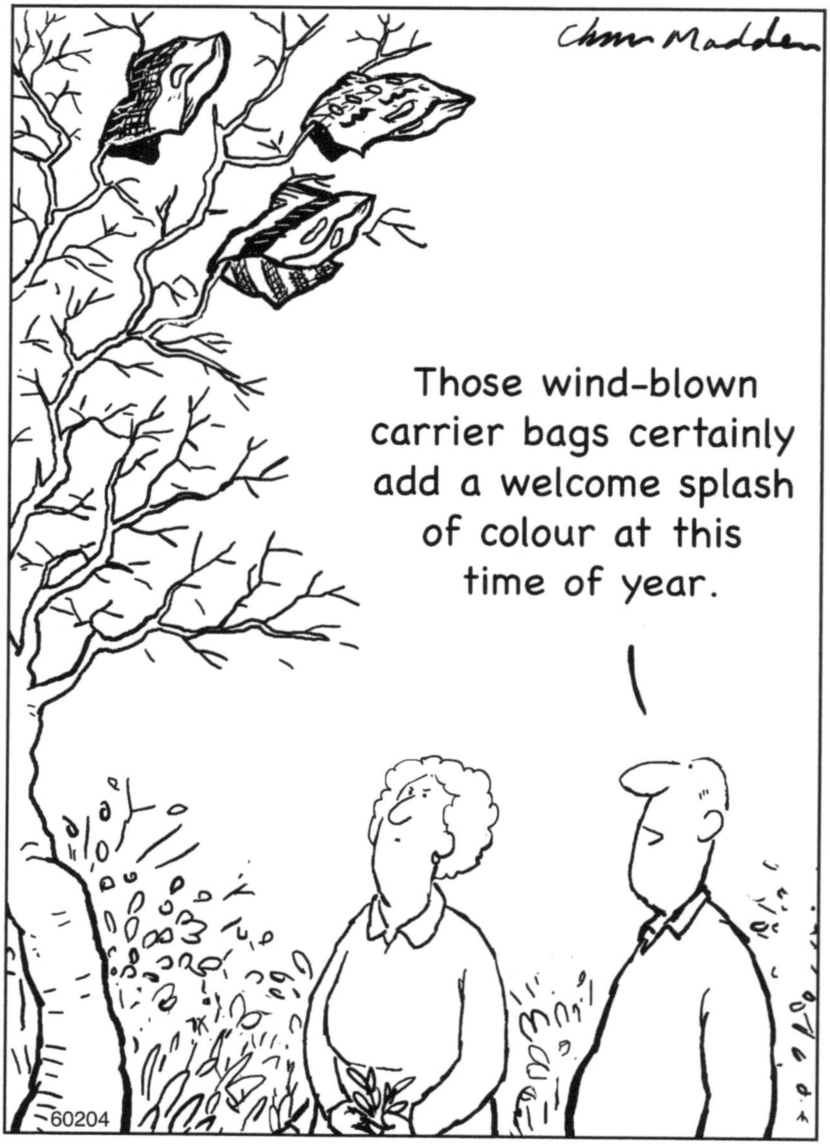
Chris Madden
Those wind-blown carrier bags certainly add a welcome splash of colour at this time of year.
60204

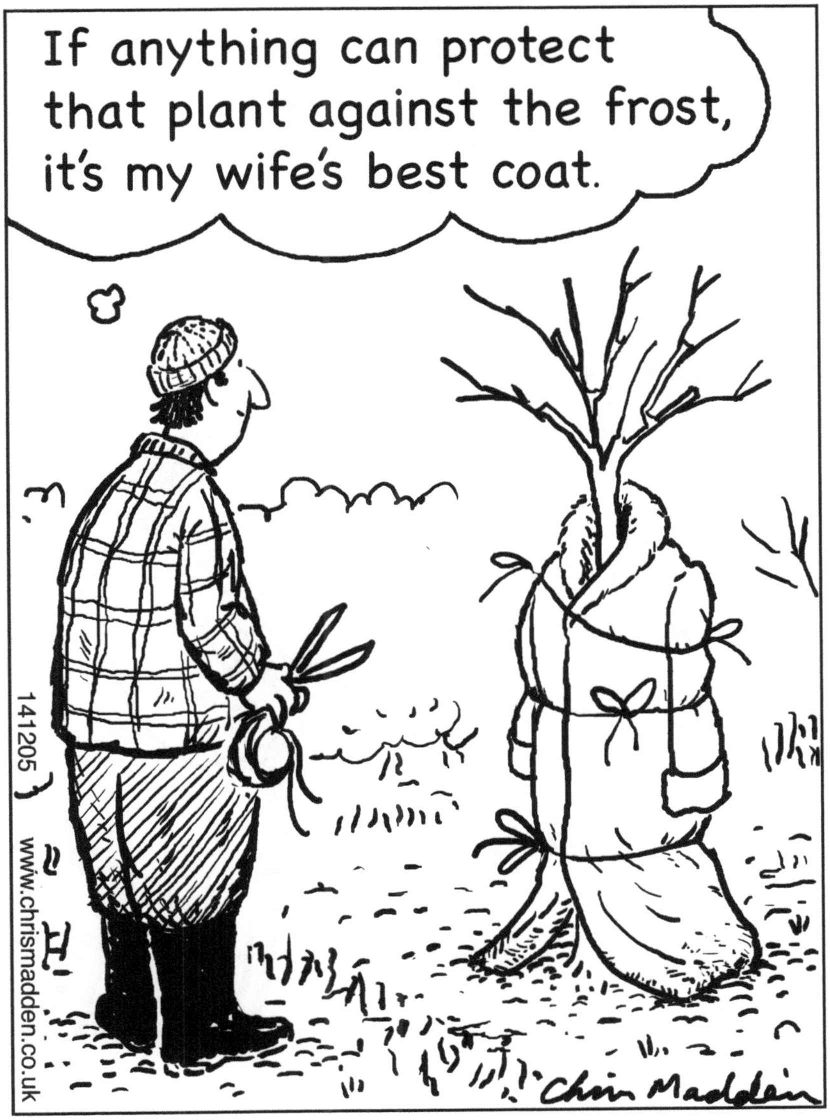
If anything can protect that plant against the frost, it's my wife's best coat.
141205
www.chrismadden.co.uk
Chris Madden

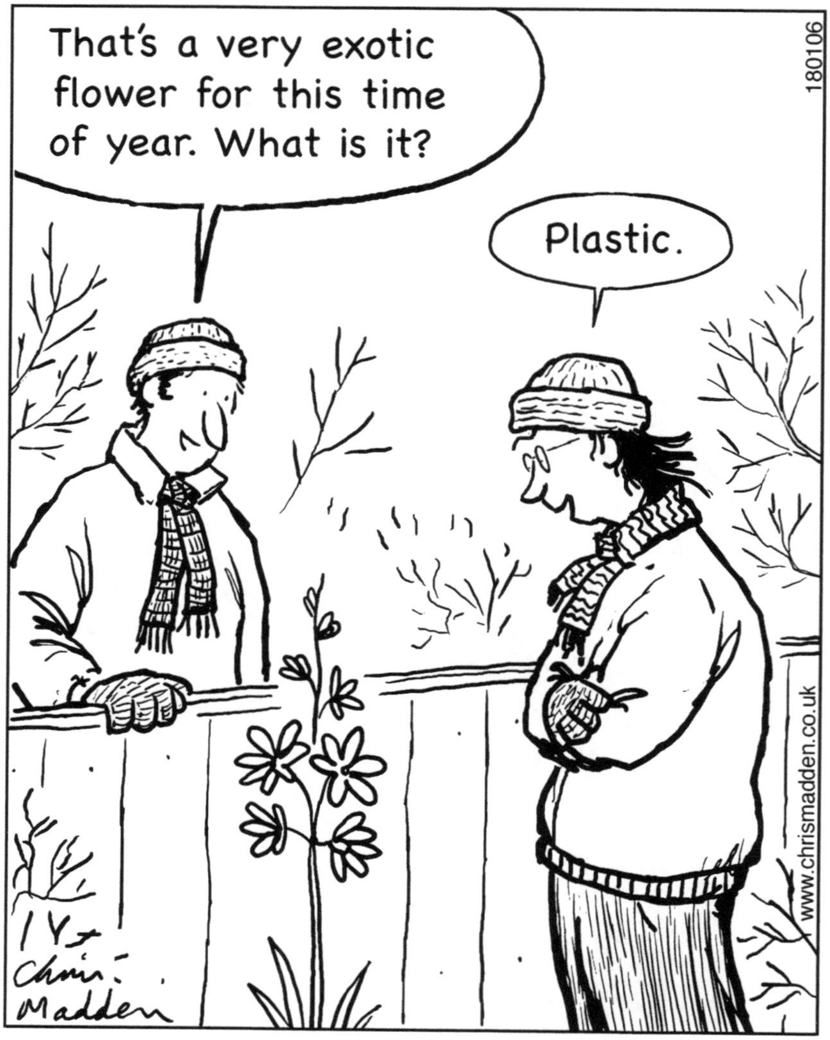
That's a very exotic flower for this time of year. What is it?
Plastic.
180106
www.chrismadden.co.uk
Chris Madden

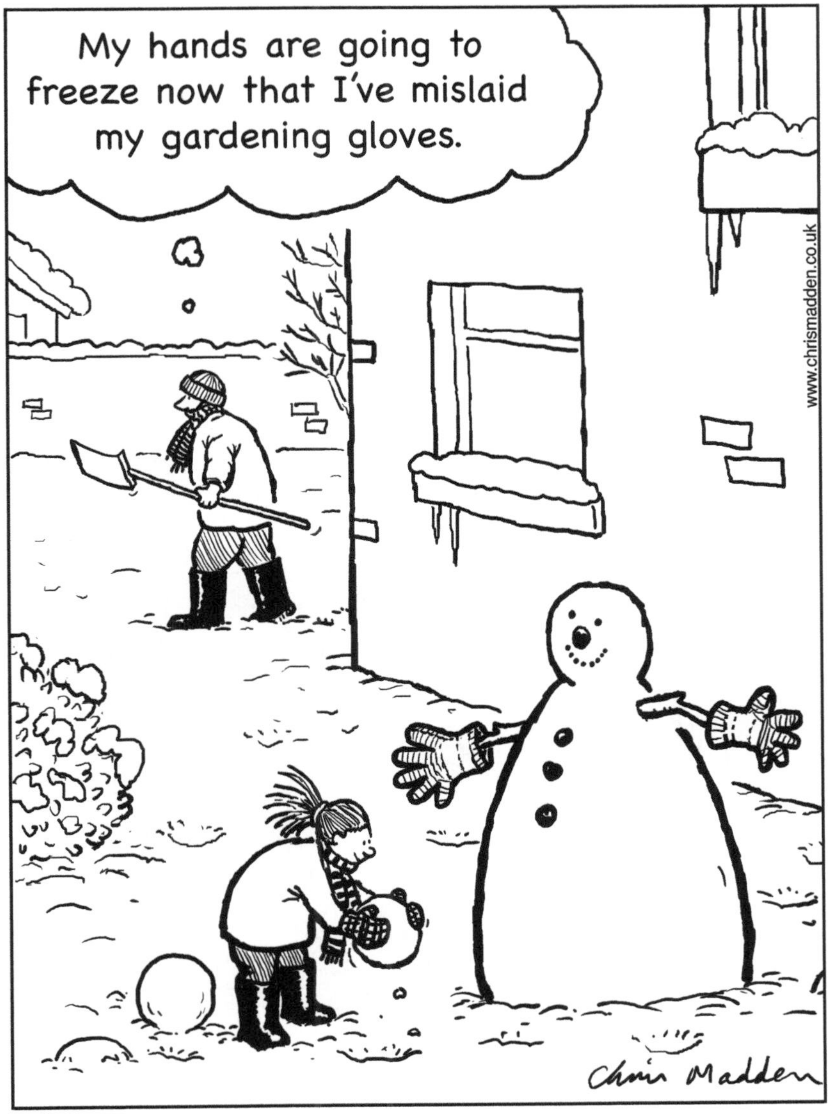
My hands are going to freeze now that I've mislaid my gardening gloves.
www.chrismadden.co.uk
Chris Madden

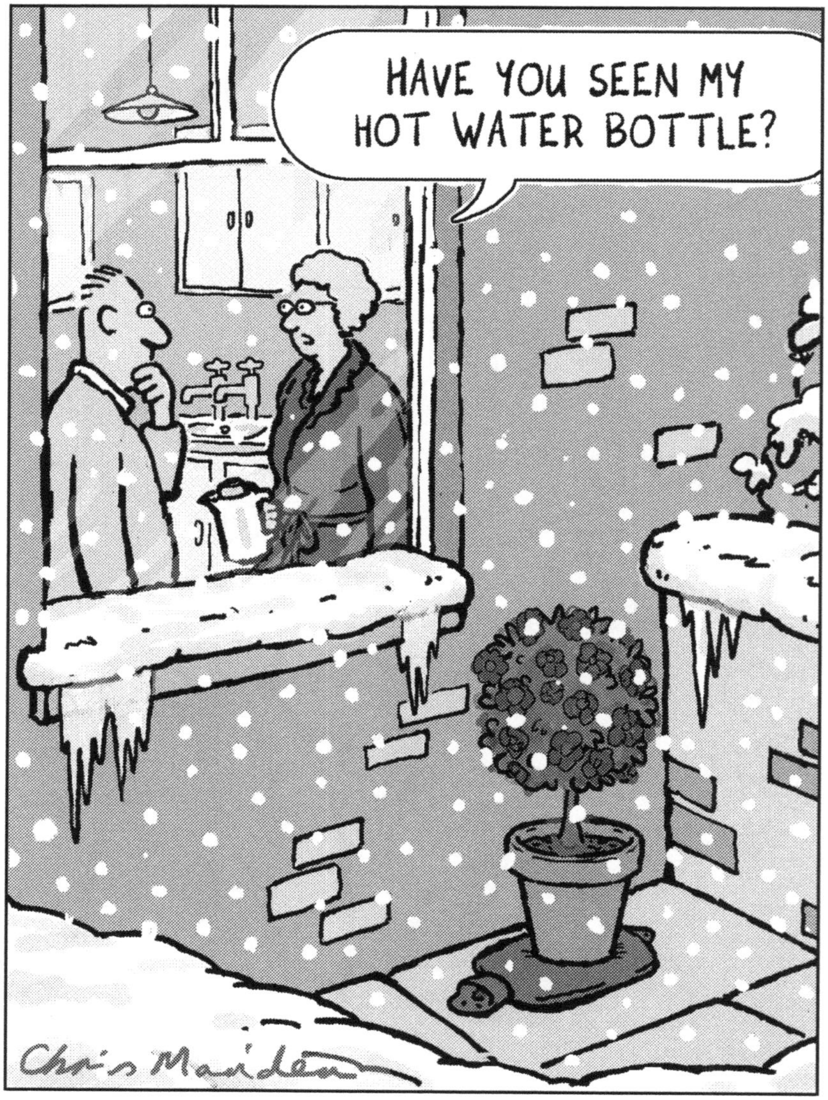
HAVE YOU SEEN MY HOT WATER BOTTLE?
Chris Madden

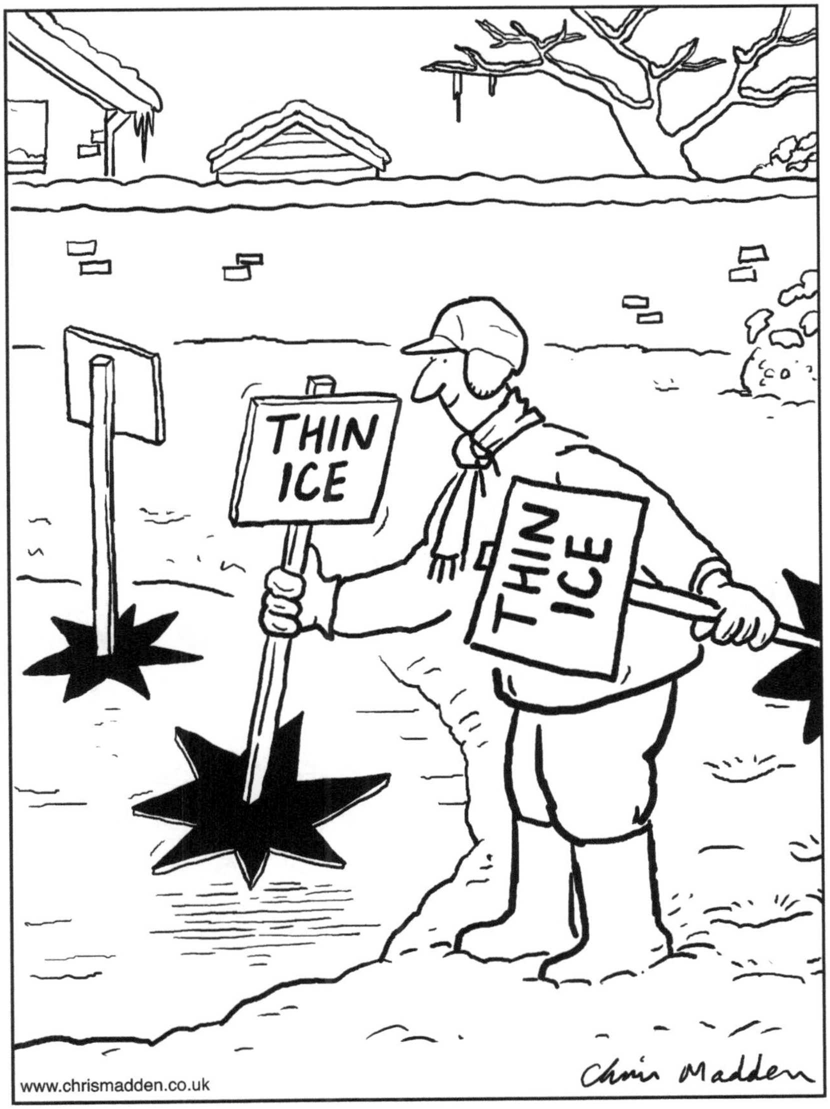
THIN ICE
THIN ICE
www.chrismadden.co.uk
Chris Madden

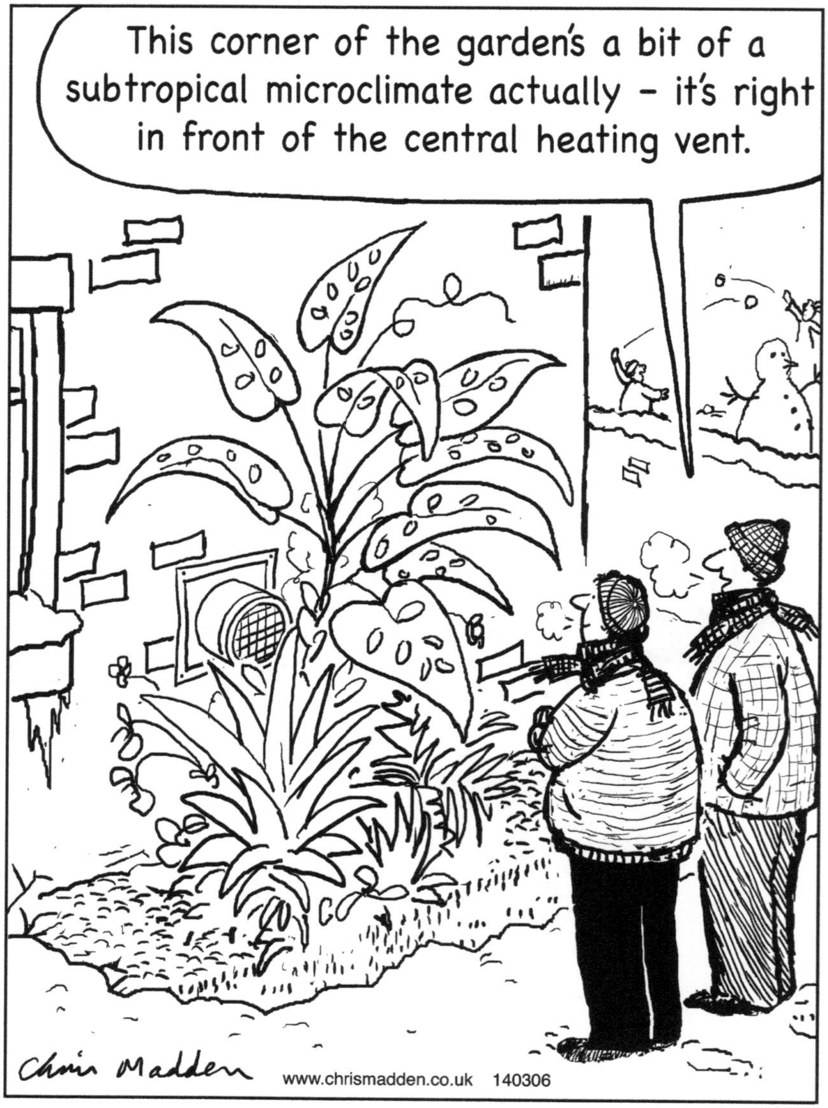
This corner of the garden's a bit of a subtropical microclimate actually – it's right in front of the central heating vent.
Chris Madden
www.chrismadden.co.uk 140306

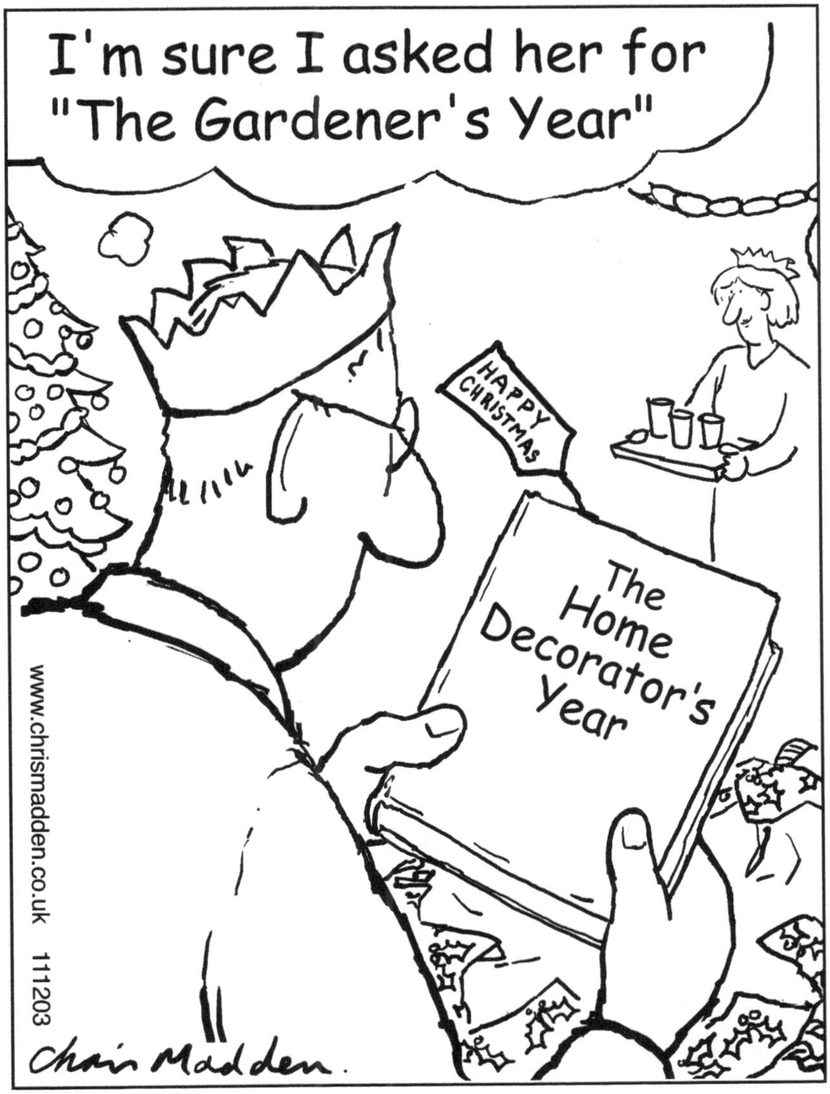
I'm sure I asked her for "The Gardener's Year"
HAPPY CHRISTMAS
The Home Decorator's Year
www.chrismadden.co.uk 111203
Chris Madden

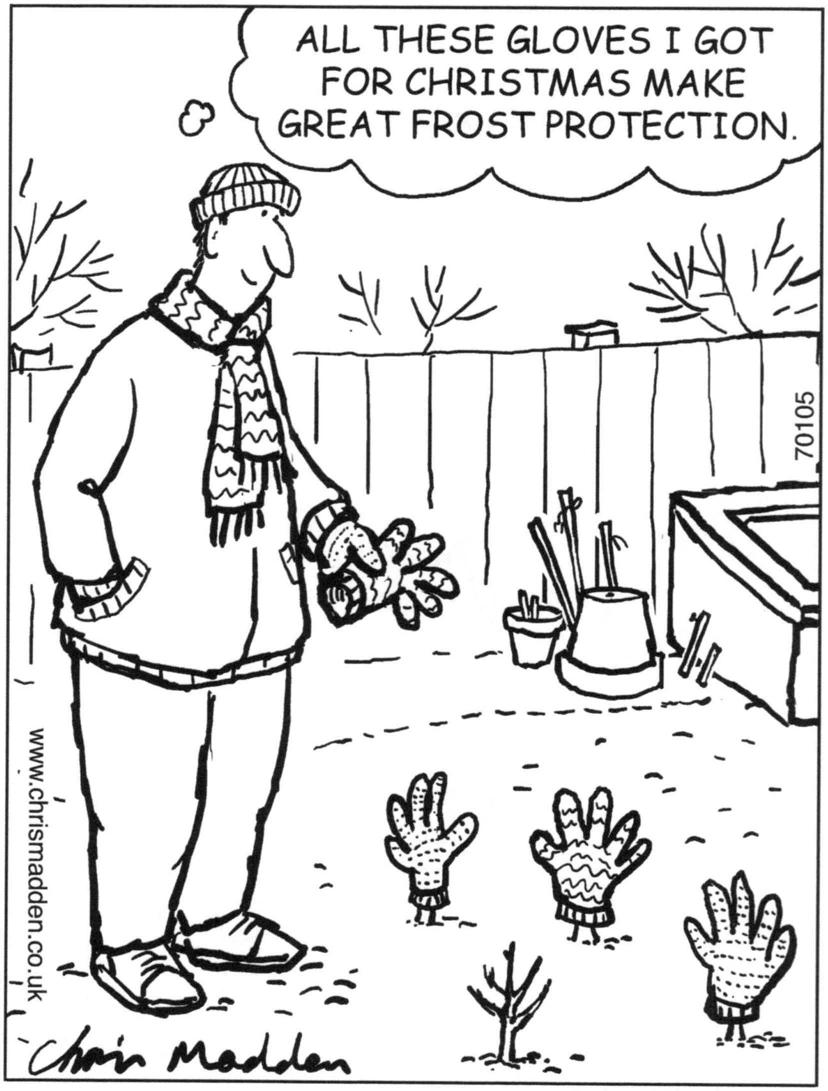
ALL THESE GLOVES I GOT FOR CHRISTMAS MAKE GREAT FROST PROTECTION.
70105
www.chrismadden.co.uk
Chris Madden

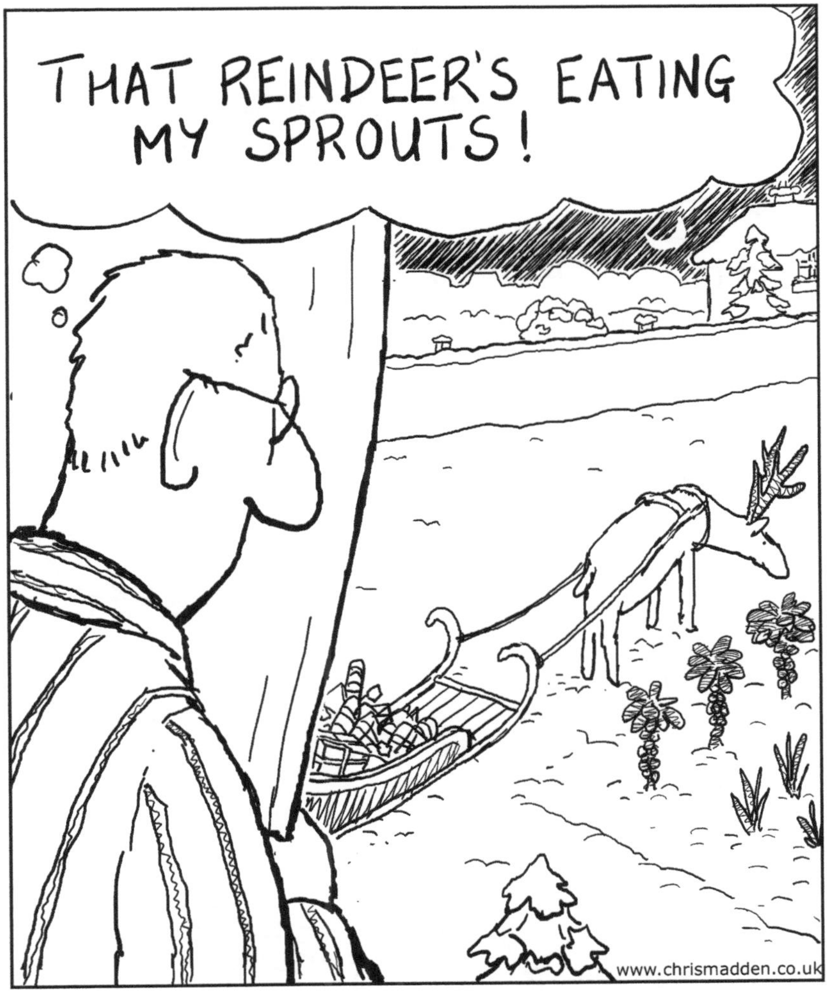
THAT REINDEER'S EATING MY SPROUTS!
www.chrismadden.co.uk

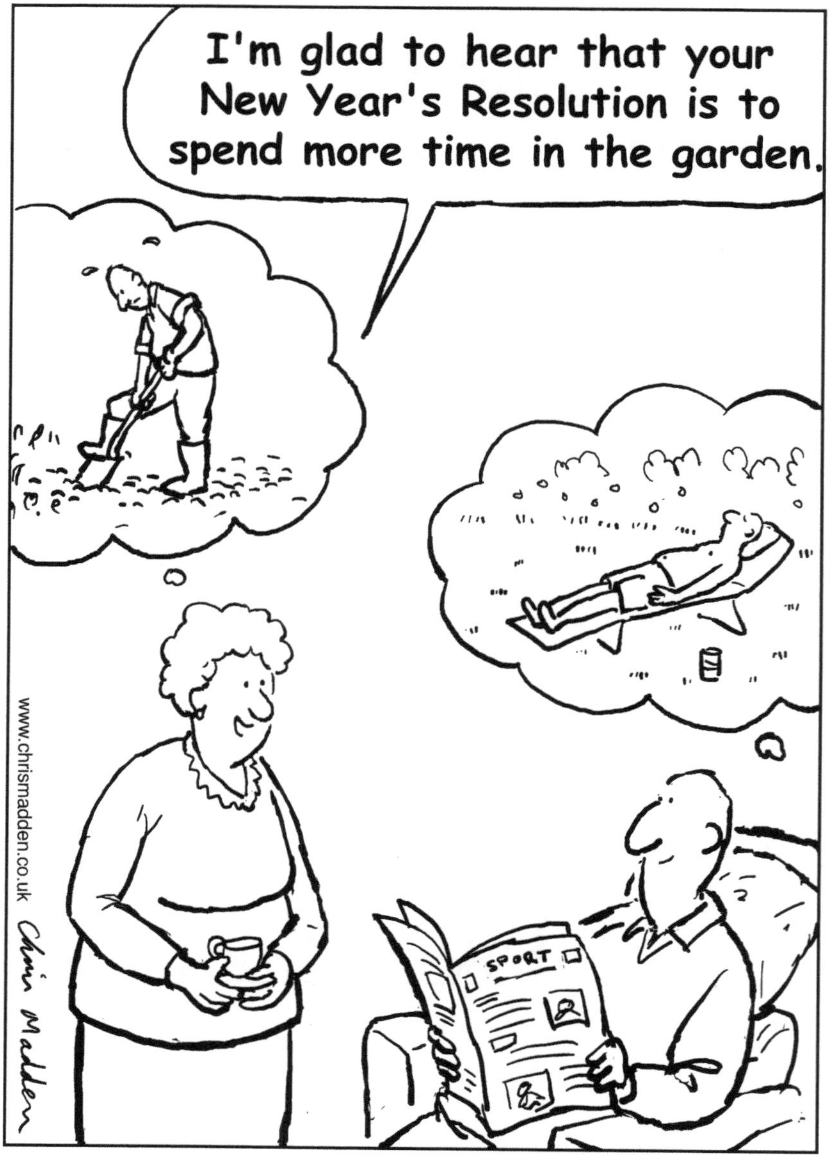
I'm glad to hear that your New Year's Resolution is to spend more time in the garden.
SPORT
www.chrismadden.co.uk
Chris Madden

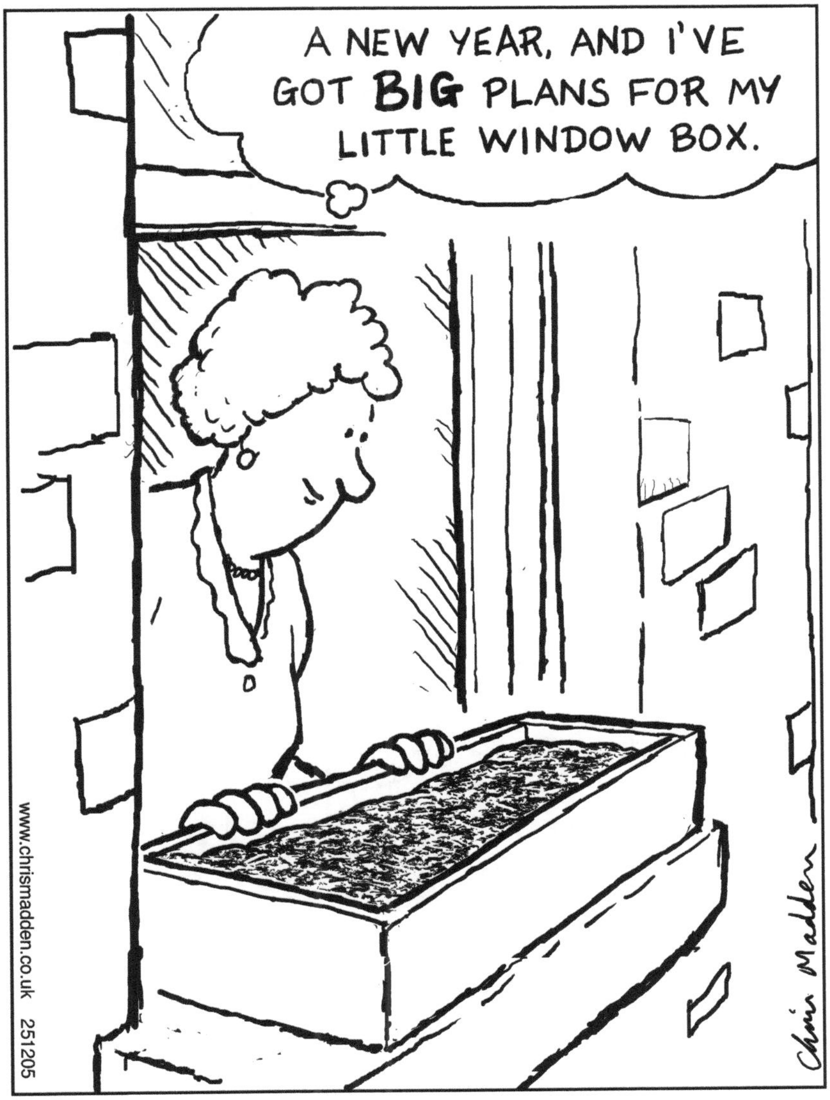
A NEW YEAR, AND I'VE GOT BIG PLANS FOR MY LITTLE WINDOW BOX.
www.chrismadden.co.uk 251205
Chris Madden

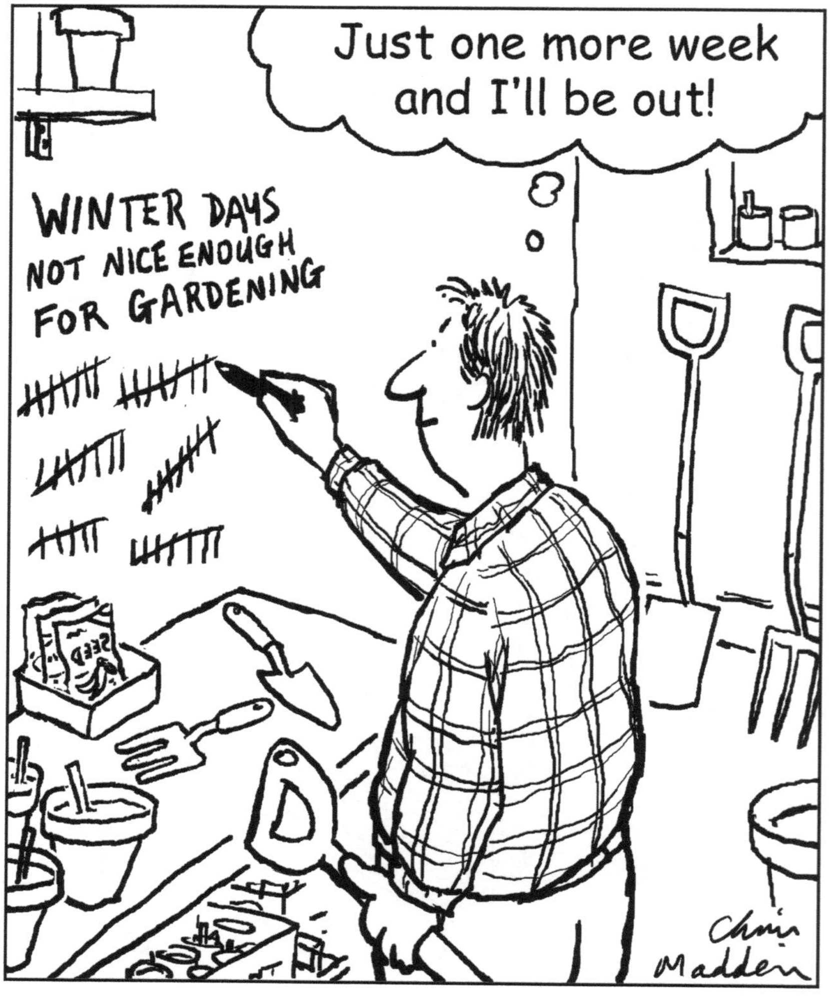
Just one more week and I'll be out!
WINTER DAYS NOT NICE ENOUGH FOR GARDENING
SEED
Chris Madden

Lightning Source UK Ltd.
Milton Keynes UK
UKHW031848161221
395703UK00006B/320